TONGUE IN CHURCH

TONGUE IN ~~CHEEK~~ CHURCH

A Liberating Primer on Christian Vocabulary

Samantha Bise

the pilgrim press

The Pilgrim Press
1300 East 9th Street
Cleveland, Ohio 44114
thepilgrimpress.com

Published 2026.

Library of Congress Cataloging-in-Publication Data on file.
LCCN: 2026937007

ISBN 978-0-8298-0770-7 (paper)
ISBN 978-0-8298-0771-4 (ebook)

Printed on acid-free paper in the United States of America.

Dedication

This book is dedicated to Dillon, Tabitha, and Sophia.

Without the three of you, this book would have been written much faster. This is a small price to pay for your company.

CONTENTS

PROLOGUE

MY GRANDMOTHER—my dad's mom—died at the beginning of the pandemic, so we could not gather for her funeral until a year after her passing. When we finally held her memorial, my dad's family gathered in the church of his childhood in a small, rural town in western Pennsylvania. My parents didn't raise me and my brothers in any religious way. My home was not atheist, but rather agnostic. After what I witnessed at my grandmother's memorial service, I understood why.

I held my first daughter, only a few months old at the time, in my arms as we sat in the pew. My husband sat to my right, my parents were in the pew directly in front of me, and my cousin and her wife sat to the right of my parents. The pastor was the son of the previous pastor, who my dad grew up hearing preach. He spent the first few minutes telling beautiful stories about my grandmother and her community service: her years of teaching Sunday School and the blankets she crocheted for those in need.

It is always comforting to hear about the generous ways your loved one spent their time here on earth. People were grieving and crying.

Then the pastor's tone shifted. My daughter was shaken awake by the slamming of his fist against the podium as he began to yell.

Memory is elusive. I don't remember how long the pastor went on like this, but I will never forget snippets of what he said—or rather, yelled—to the church full of crying people mourning the loss of their mother, mother-in-law, sister, aunt, grandmother, great-grandmother, great-great-grandmother, and friend.

He said that if we wanted to see her again, we had to repent. He told us to come up to the front of the church and confess Jesus as our Lord and savior right now, or we would never see her again in heaven. He went on to say that we would suffer for eternity if we did not believe in Jesus. He even made a comment about Genesis, stating that God created Adam and Eve, not Adam and Steve—which is when my shock was broken. I looked at my cousin and her wife, angry on their behalf.

Around the church I saw family members—my grandfather, aunts, uncles, and cousins—nodding their head in agreement with the pastor. They had their hands in the air, and I heard a few members of my family affirming, "Praise Jesus."

My husband and I looked at each other in disbelief. I looked at my parents in the pew in front of me, who were staring straight ahead, expressionless. They were among the very few who were unimpressed with this pastor's performance, and I had never been so proud to be their child.

I was twenty-eight years old the first time I walked into a church and meant it. That was three years before my grandmother's memorial. The words and phrases this pastor used were the same words I had grown accustomed to hearing in the mainline Protestant churches I had attended over those years, and yet, these words meant something very different to him and my western Pennsylvania family members. I realized that, although we all consider ourselves Christians, we were using words like "repent," "Lord," "Savior," and "believe" very differently. We are speaking a different language using the same words.

I came home from my grandmother's memorial determined to learn everything I could about religious and Christian language. I earned my doctorate in Literacy, Culture, and Language Education from Indiana University; my dissertation research focused on the ways people understand some biblical language. I read every book I could find about the Hebrew and Greek languages and the various processes of translating the Bible. I began taking classes at my local seminary. This book is a collection of what I have learned over the years about the meanings hidden in Christian vocabulary—and how those meanings, when understood, can liberate church language from the abuses of judgment, control, and domination.

IN THE BEGINNING

Some people read the Bible as if under a microscope: up close and seeing only snippets of it at a time. Certainly this way of approaching the Bible can be beautiful and deeply transformative, connecting with a verse or story that feels true to their lives and circumstances. Yet microscopic view lacks some perspective that only a telescopic view can offer. Zooming out and seeing the entire story from a distance offers context that is essential for understanding Christian language at large. Similarly, the way people read the Bible is informed by their understandings of God. Some read the Bible as if the concept of God is an invented, outdated, magical figment of ancient imagination. Others read it as if God is a concrete, historical, completely knowable person in our lives.

However we conceive of God now, people were experiencing the divine in biblical times, too. They wrote about their experiences of God, and the language they used to describe these experiences was shaped by their time and place: specific cultures, economic circumstances, political systems, power structures, and the perspectives of individuals and communities. In biblical times like in modern times, language points to the powers at work in society—not only through vocabulary but through overtone, often set by those who control a society's money and policies. Words like "welfare" and "tax relief" today, for example, show economic power at work. "Welfare," referring to economic assistance for low-income individuals and families, is often framed negatively in political discourse. However, "tax relief," referring to economic assistance that typically benefits businesses and higher-income individuals, is often framed positively. This dynamic can be found culturally, too. Assertive women are often called "bossy," while assertive men are often called "leaders." Language is not neutral. It exposes—and reinforces—who holds power and who is disempowered.

There are power dynamics hidden inside church language and the Bible—both oppressive powers and liberating powers—and once we recognize them, we cannot unsee them. At its core, Christianity is not an oppressive power, however we cannot deny or ignore the fact that throughout history and the present day, Christianity has embraced sociopolitical power structures and oppressed many people. Examining the linguistic, social, and cultural origins of Christian terminology helps us excavate the church's foundational identity, which is rooted in resistance to, rebellion against, and revolution from dominant power structures. A lot of church language was originally tongue-in-cheek—a way to mock, ridicule, and resist power structures. Many words and phrases we use in church today first held seriously irreverent intentions.

One example can be found in Jesus healing the demoniacs (Matthew 8:28-34, Mark 5:1-20, and Luke 8:26-39). It's important to remember that the Gospels were written in Greek; in Greek psychology, emotion was often referred to as a *daimon*. Somebody taken over by strong emotion, like anger or fear, was said to be possessed by a *daimon*. Additionally, this story is set in northern Israel near where a Roman legion (large military unit) was stationed.

In this story, a sick man appears to be in emotional turmoil and is said to be possessed. He says that his turmoil is caused by a "legion." When Jesus tells the demon to come out of the man, the demon names itself as "Legion." The story hides its true meaning in plain sight—the presence of Roman soldiers is demonic, evil, and oppressive in nature. The man's emotional suffering is being caused by the nearby Roman army, and Jesus's healing of the man is a tongue-in-cheek way of critiquing the Roman Empire. This makes sense, given that the Roman Empire conquered Canaan, Jesus's home, and was oppressing many Jews.

Understanding the context behind the word "legion" helps us see this story from a wider perspective—a perspective that incorporates the particular social, economic, cultural, and political context of Jesus's lifetime. Jesus did not exist outside of this context; he did not float divinely beyond and untouched by the world in which he lived. Jesus was God incarnate, living in human flesh. Jesus, like us, existed within the dynamics of the specific time and place he was born into—including the dynamics of language. Some of this language has deeper meaning when we explore its social, economic, cultural, and political context.

For example, before Jesus, many Roman emperors were called the Son of God. To refer to Jesus as the Son of God put Jesus in direct opposition to the Roman emperor—a turn of phrase with intentional and serious implications. Jesus knew his message ran contrary to the dominant powers of his day. He spoke out against authorities who favored legalism over compassion. He criticized social norms by engaging in activities that were deemed taboo, like sharing meals with outcasts and sinners. Jesus also knew that you can get away with a lot by communicating in metaphors and by hiding his countercultural message in common phrases. A wink, an indirect parable, a snippet of coded language: these were tools to communicate effectively with those seeking liberation from Rome's control. Jews and Gentiles alike in Jesus's time would have understood the rebellious overtones.

The overarching story told in the Bible is about God guiding people to liberation, and it is only preserved because of language. Today, a Christian community who is collectively unaware of their tradition's history in using language to align boldly against oppressive powers is at risk of misusing that same language to become an oppressive power itself. *Tongue in Church* explores the many ways that power has influenced the language of the church in order to rescue it from literal interpretations that dull its liberating intent, beginning with the book through which many of these words and phrases have been passed down to us: the Bible.

BIBLICAL LANGUAGE

Understanding the historical context of biblical language and Christian vocabulary is vital. After all, religion is made up of words: sacred texts, liturgies, creeds, rituals, and prayer. But when hijacked and misapplied, all that language can become dull and lose its edge—or worse, its purpose. Many words and phrases throughout the Bible have been and continue to be misinterpreted when the linguistic history of the Bible is not taken into account. This includes the Church's role in shaping, preserving, interpreting, and even controlling biblical language. When Christians today claim that having a Bible-based faith means reading the Bible literally, they claim a fallacy. Biblical language often contains meanings that are lost when read only for literal understanding. To take the Bible seriously, as we will see, requires us to go deeper into the world of church words. When we explore the text of the Bible, we simultaneously explore the worlds lived in by the biblical storytellers, writers, translators, and audiences. To understand the meanings of biblical language, therefore, requires an understanding of the Bible's original context and the history of its translation. Behind every word is an entire world to be exposed.

Biblical texts were created, retold, and written down before Christianity existed as a formal expression of faith, so biblical language comes out of cultures ranging from the eleventh century BCE to approximately 130 CE. For this reason, I distinguish between "biblical language"—words and phrases that come to us from the texts written before 130 CE—and "church language" words and phrases that come to us from communities of believers after the biblical texts were written. While these distinctions are not hard-and-fast, we will use them as a guide for the placement of words in one category or the other. For example, the word "Bible" is not in the Bible and is therefore church language rather than biblical language. As we explore the linguistic contexts of both the Bible and of the Church, we start by unpacking the word "Bible."

The Greek root for the word *Bible* means "little books," and that is exactly what the Bible is—a collection of little books bound together and widely distributed. The first part of the Bible is a collection of Hebrew texts, often called the Old Testament or the Hebrew Bible. These texts belong, first and foremost, to the Jewish people and their faith. It's important to know that the Hebrew Bible/Old Testament used in Christian communities isn't identical to the Hebrew Bible/Tanakh used by Jewish communities; there are differences in the number and order of books as well as in the interpretation. The second part of the Bible, generally called the New Testament, is unique to Christianity and includes texts about Jesus.

The first five books of the Bible—Genesis, Exodus, Leviticus, Numbers, and Deuteronomy—are known in Judaism as the *Torah*. The Hebrew word *torah* often gets translated as "law," but another appropriate translation is "teaching." Christians also refer to these five books as the *Pentateuch*, which simply means "five books." In addition to the

Torah, the Hebrew Bible also contains the *Nevi'im*, meaning "prophets," and the *Ketuvim*, meaning "writings." Scholars think the oldest passages from the Hebrew Bible come from between the 11th to 8th centuries BCE. Daniel is the latest written book of the Hebrew Bible, and it comes from the second century BCE.

The New Testament is written by a handful of Jesus followers between about the 50s into the 120s CE. For context, it is widely agreed that Jesus was born around 4 BCE and was murdered in the early 30s CE. The first New Testament writings were from or about Paul, whose letters began to circulate in the 50s CE to diaspora communities—Christian communities who dispersed after the destruction of Jerusalem. The Gospel of Mark, likely written by somebody with limited formal education as evidenced by its use of elementary Greek, was written in 70–71 CE; the Gospels of Matthew and Luke were written around 90–100 CE; and the Gospel of John was written around 100–120 CE. Mark, Matthew, and Luke are called the Synoptic Gospels; Synoptic is Greek for "viewed together." The Synoptic Gospels are distinct from the style and content of the Gospel of John. It is generally agreed that all four Gospels were written around or after the year 70 CE (with some arguing that Mark may have been written slightly earlier), which is the year the Roman Empire took back Jerusalem after the First Jewish Revolt.

Even the earliest copies that we have found of biblical texts don't agree with each other and have variations. Since the second century, Christians have known that manuscripts of biblical texts have discrepancies. Since the third century, Christian theologians have debated over and doubted that Paul wrote the Letter to the Hebrews. People have been translating the Bible since the third century BCE, and nearly every translation since has built upon previous translations. The language of the Bible reminds me of "military brats"—people who grew up with a parent in the military. They move so much in their childhood that it becomes difficult to answer the question, "Where are you from?" Their answer is usually an explanation rather than a single hometown or state. Asking what language the Bible calls "home" is similarly difficult.

The Hebrew Bible was originally written in Hebrew. The New Testament was written in Greek. Jesus spoke in Aramaic. This means his words were translated before the Gospels were even written down the first time. Right away, translation is playing a role in the story handed down to us. The Greek translation of the Hebrew Bible is called the Septuagint. Greek was the lingua franca of the Roman Empire; however, the New Testament was not written in classical Greek but rather in common Greek—now referred to as Koine Greek. To further complicate things, the ancient Greeks did not have punctuation as we understand it today.

St. Jerome translated the Hebrew Bible and New Testament into Latin in the fourth century. We call his translation the Latin Vulgate. Jerome's Vulgate was not entirely well received. For example, a congregation rioted over the Latin translation of Jonah 4:6 stating that Jonah was covered by the shadow of a gourd rather than ivy. People become attached to the details and their own understandings of sacred texts; this was true in Jerome's time, and it is true now.

Biblical translations don't stop with the Vulgate. The invention of the printing press in the mid-fifteenth century set the stage for the wider distribution of Bibles. The Reformation significantly focused on the translation of the Bible into the languages of the people. Among others, Martin Luther translated the Bible into German in the 1500s. Since then, we have had thousands of translations. Many biblical translations may more accurately be called paraphrases, rephrasing the language of an earlier translation. The United States Bible Society (UBS) states that the Bible has been translated into about 700 languages. Most of these languages have one version of the Bible—except in English, which has a variety of published translations of the Bible.

Even the difference in a biblical text's written format impacts our modern understanding of its meaning. Biblical texts that first existed in oral traditions made great use of poetry, alliteration, and other tools intended for the ear rather than the eye. Ancient Hebrew stories and teachings included the repetition of words and phrases to aid the listener's memorization. When these texts were finally put down onto scrolls, the writing prioritized literacy in listening not in reading. Jesus was a Jewish man who referred to the Hebrew scriptures often, so their linguistic style—the familiar repetition and rhythm that his audiences knew—is an important factor to understand Jesus's teachings.

In contrast, nearly every New Testament manuscript was a codex, not a scroll. A codex is written on separate sheets fastened together, like a book, while a scroll is written in long columns. The codex format was used like a notebook to jot down notes or preserve records, not to publish fully formed thoughts and elaborate literature. The codex was useful for quickly transferring information, which was useful across the early Christian diaspora. Yet the format affirms scholarly consensus: authors of New Testament texts were not aware they were writing for future audiences for centuries to come.

The history of which books are in the Bible is complicated. While the books of the Hebrew scriptures had been largely settled by the first century BCE, what was to be included in the New Testament was not established until the fourth century. In 398 CE, a group of Christian bishops gathered in Hippo Regius (on the northern tip of Africa in modern-day Algeria) to determine which Gospels and letters were considered authoritative. Apocryphal and extra-canonical gospels, letters, and other writings were excluded from the final canon of the New Testament for various reasons—including theological disagreements, questions about authorship, undermining of hierarchical church structures, and Gnostic or non-orthodox views.

For example, the Gospel of Thomas was not included because it emphasizes salvation through self-knowledge. The Gospel of Mary challenges gender roles by presenting Mary Magdalene as a key disciple; the Gospel of Judas contradicts orthodox interpretations of Judas as a betrayer; and the Gospel of Philip hints at a potential romantic relationship between Jesus and Mary Magdalene. Another example is the Apocrypha, which is a collection of Jewish writings written about two centuries before Jesus. *Apocrypha* comes from the Greek adjective *apokryphos*, which means "private," and the Greek verb *apokryptein*, which means "to hide away." The Apocrypha was "hidden away" from many printings of the Bible—sometimes to save printers money by including fewer pages in each Bible. Other ancient texts were excluded from the Bible as we know it today, yet they circulated widely before canonization was solidified in the fourth century.

The Bible is a constant work in progress, and choices made throughout history impact the text we read today. For example, the Codex Bobiensis is one of the oldest surviving Latin manuscripts of the New Testament, and it contains a difference in the Lord's Prayer. Instead of "Let your kingdom come," it reads "I have come to your kingdom." These are two very different statements! Another example: Matthew 17:21 is missing from many Bible translations. This verse was not part of the original New Testament and was later added in, so many translators now remove the verse in an attempt to keep the Bible as true to the original as possible. If your Bible is missing Matthew 17:21, you have a translation that is more closely translated to the original texts. The Bible is to be pondered, wrestled with, and even argued with—not just its meaning but also its content and construction. This is an authentic expression of faith.

In the mid-nineteenth century, Christianity was up against the culture's growing sense of reason, rationalism, and science. To combat this, Catholics declared the Pope "infallible" and many Protestants deemed the Bible "inerrant." The assertion that the Bible contains solely literal truths is a very new Christian belief. It is also a significant reason why many post-Christian adults reject the Christianity of their childhoods: they cannot reconcile the contradicting truths in their "inerrant" Bibles with scientific truths and diverse worldviews.

Certain sects of modern Christians identify themselves as "biblical" Christians, asserting the Bible's inerrancy. To be clear—Christian beliefs and practices have never been contained by the Bible alone and have always extended beyond these texts. As a Christian, I don't understand what a "Bible-believing Christian" means. The Bible has always been a living document, a work in progress. As culture evolves, our language evolves with it; as language evolves, translations of the Bible also evolve. Jewish people, and a growing number of Christians, view scripture as a complex text to enter into and engage with rather than an instruction manual to pledge your allegiance to. I will go so far as to call this level of allegiance to the Bible "idolatry." It can help point to understandings God, but it is not God.

Clearly, we could be debilitated by how complex this ancient collection of texts is—or we could enter into the complexity and stay curious. To do this, we must choose a translation we can actually read. I use the New Revised Standard Version (NRSV) when I am quoting directly from the Bible, unless otherwise noted, for many reasons. The NRSV is ecumenical, meaning scholars from various denominations and faiths worked on this translation together—including Catholic, Orthodox, Protestant, and Jewish scholars. So the NRSV is not the product of only one Christian denomination's view of the Bible, and it includes Jewish voices which are vital when translating the Hebrew Bible. Additionally, the NRSV was translated directly from the original biblical sources and from the original Hebrew and Greek, unlike some other Bible versions.

Even so, English translations of the Bible bring their own language history and power structures to the biblical text. English did not begin as the language of power and commerce it is today, but instead as a language of the common folk. In fact, there was a time when servants spoke English and masters spoke French. Servants would speak English when working, but would switch to French when communicating with their masters. This is why some of our fancier words are influenced by French. For example, "mansion" simply means house in French, but in English it means large house. The English language was influenced by French power, and it shows. Language is always influenced by those in power.

An economic collapse around the 1400s put more visible reliance on the working class and English-speaking population. During this crisis, it became clear that, without the working class, there was no economic way forward for the wider society. This reckoning allowed people to move "up" into another socioeconomic class for the first time and, with the invention of the printing press, created the desire to speak "correctly"—whatever that means—in an effort to climb the socioeconomic ladder. The first English grammar guide was published in 1586, and the printing press enabled its wide distribution. People began to use this apparently agreed-upon style of English,, and the language gained power. In a short period of time, English was standardized and the first dictionary was published. Language began to be seen as a static, straightforward tool of economy rather than a living, breathing process of communication. The Bible has similarly come to be viewed as static, though this is not how the Bible or language works.

Language demands flexibility for its ever-evolving and versatile nature. As an example, my toddler has been practicing using the word "cut." Our pizza cutter broke years ago, and we haven't gotten around to replacing it. Instead, we use scissors to cut our pizza into slices—a domestic trick I highly recommend. Then my toddler got her first haircut. Now she pretends to cut my hair with her fingers, saying, "I am going to cut you like pizza!" She has experienced the use of cutting in the context of pizza and hair, so this makes sense to her. Language requires context and maturity to grasp.

Many words can be used in various contexts. The English word "run" can be used to refer to running out of time, a nose running, running a meeting, running for president, running for exercise, etc. This word means something different depending on its context. To assume that every possible definition is at play any time the word "run" is used is called "illegitimate totality transfer." This is important when we discuss biblical and church words. There is value in looking at the history and origins of a word, as I do throughout this book. However, words adapt over time, developing new or additional meanings. This book does not claim that "old" meanings are the only meanings of words, but I argue that examining the history of a word in its historical and cultural context can help us go deeper into our Christianity. Lexicographers track the evolution of language, deciding what words to edit, take out, or add to dictionaries. The simple fact that dictionaries shift with time demonstrates the ability of language to mutate in creative ways—giving language more meaning, not less. The dictionary is not dogma, and neither is the Bible.

The desire for an inerrant Bible that is the authoritative Word of God is significantly related to power and its desire for controlled stability. A text that is seen as the ultimate authority on ethical, moral, political, and spiritual matters can—and has—led to harmful applications of biblical interpretation. Often, those who align with puritanical interpretations are people invested in positions of power, and they enforce their interpretations to maintain that power, consciously or not. As history teaches us, power and corruption go hand-in-hand. The Bible, however, with its freedom stories from exodus to resurrection, cannot be read well by those who prefer power and control.

To understand the Bible, one must enter into the complexities that accompany the volume's language. Some people prefer a biblical translation that is closer to the original Hebrew or Greek, but this is also problematic. To translate this way would be nearly incomprehensible in modern English. The cultural presumptions of life in the first century are not the cultural presumptions of contemporary life. Language, its meanings and context, have changed in ways that can make such direct translation unhelpful to today's readers. Reading the Bible immerses us in the linguistic complexity of this ancient collection of books.

Adam and Eve

The debate about the factual validity of the Book of Genesis used to anger me, because there is literally a talking snake. However, the older I get and the more mature my faith becomes, the less attention I give to this debate. Humans are, after all, meaning-making creatures, and I am on a search for meaning that transforms and liberates.

The Adam and Eve story borrows from the Epic of Gilgamesh, a tale from ancient Mesopotamia that predates Genesis. Genesis and the Epic of Gilgamesh have many commonalities. As it relates to Adam and Eve, both stories have humans being created from clay. In the Epic of Gilgamesh, Ut-napishtim and his wife desire to become like gods, similar to Adam and Eve, resulting in their exile from a garden. Additionally, Eden is suspected to come from the Sumerians.

The Adam and Eve story aligns with Exodus—not surprising when we realize that the book of Exodus was written before Genesis. In Exodus, it is clear that if the Israelites disobeyed God they would be kicked out of their land. In Genesis, Adam and Eve disobeyed God and were kicked out of the garden. The parallel stories share a point: to live in a land of peace requires obedience to God. Another way to think about obedience to God is to be in alignment with God.

Reading the Genesis text through its many translations provides a lens for making meaning from the differing creation stories. There has never been one understanding of this complex book, so we engage its complexity with curiosity to see what we could be missing. In Adam and Eve's story, we have the infamous tree of knowledge of good and evil. Good and evil in Hebrew are tob and ra, which translate to pleasure and pain. Eating from this tree results in not knowing pleasure without pain, or pain without pleasure. In Genesis chapters 2 through 4, Adam and Eve are living in the Garden of Eden, then God kicks them out, and their son Cain kills their other son Abel. In Hebrew, Adam means humanity; Eve means life; Eden means delight; Cain means spear; and Abel means fleeting breath, or something that is there one moment and gone the next. These translations clarify a deeper meaning in the text.

Considering the story with the original Hebrew in mind allows us to see ourselves reflected in it. We are born into a certain innocence—a garden of delights, if you will. Eventually, we must grow up and face our own trials and troubles. It's the only path towards transformation. This process of growing up can sometimes feel abrupt, as being kicked out of childhood or the garden of delights. Perhaps we can think of Cain's killing of his brother Abel as a type of surrender to the fact that troubles will come and they will go, like our fleeting breath. The talking snake and the Hebrew meaning of the names suggest that this story is more poetic rather than a literal telling of history or strict God-ordained gender roles.

◇◇◇

Adonai

The Hebrew forefather Abraham was initially a resident of Sumer, a culture with multiple gods. Centuries later, the Exodus story begins with Moses; his experiences hearing the one God was the beginning of monotheism—a faith with one God—as we know it today. However, this God needed a name for Moses to be able to tell the Hebrews of this God.

God tells Moses that God's name is *YHWH.* Ancient Hebrew was written without vowels, so when we try to pronounce *YHWH* we find ourselves breathing in and out, making the sound of breath. Many scholars, pastors, and believers make connections between this name for God and the breath of life.

For much of history, *YHWH* was seen as too sacred to say out loud, so Jews did not say it or even write it. In many versions of the Bible, LORD is written in all caps to draw the reader's attention to the fact that something interesting was happening with this word. LORD often appears in our Old Testaments in place of *YHWH.* Instead of saying the sacred name of *YHWH,* the people would say *Adonai,* which means "the Lord." Some refused even to say *Adonai,* instead saying *ha-Shem,* meaning "the Name." This practice continues among some Jews today.

Apocalypse

The word *apocalypse* is most associated with the Book of Revelation, but this word doesn't appear in the Revelation itself. Apocalypse is the Greek title of the book, meaning "revelation" or "unveiling," but the book doesn't use the word *apocalypse* the way modern English speakers tend to mean it as "end of the world." Most English Bibles translate *apokalypsis* as "revelation," not "apocalypse." It has little to do with the future end of the world; instead, it is more about seeing through the screen and having clear insights about current circumstances.

There are many words that come to mind when we think of apocalypse, including end times, eschatology, Armageddon, and millennium. The phrase "end times" does not exist in English translations of the Bible. However, there is much conservative Christian discourse surrounding the end times and the second coming of Jesus. The word *eschatology* comes from the Greek word meaning "last" or "final," and the suffix *-ology*, which means "study" or "discourse." Eschatology literally means the "study of the last things." The word *Armageddon* is a Hebrew word that means "the mountains of Megiddo," a city in Israel[1] where many battles discussed in the Hebrew Bible took place. In the Bible, millennium means a thousand years. This can be read literally, but this literal understanding may miss some important meaning the writers of scripture may have been trying to convey. My four-year-old recently learned the number 100, and anything that is old is associated with the number 100. She thinks that I am 100-years-old. I don't correct her. I know she is not speaking literally, but instead using numbers to convey that to her, I am old. We often confuse when to take time or numbers literally and when to understand that there is more meaning behind a number.

No matter what language is associated with the apocalypse, it is a word closely connected to the Book of Revelation meaning unveiling or revelation rather than the end of the world. Apocalypse also shows up in the Bible in other books, and almost never refers to the end of the world. Instead, it often means a revealing of divine truths. For example, Simeon's prophecy about Jesus in Luke 2:32 uses the word revelation, or *apokalypsis*, to mean the revealing of God's plan to everyone, including non-Jews. Similarly, 1 Corinthians 1:7 uses this word to refer to waiting for Christ to be revealed and 1 Peter 1:13 uses this word to point to hope rather than destruction.

The author of Revelation identified himself as John. Scholars debate the identity of John because the writer of Revelation and John the Gospel writer have very different writing styles. Wherever you stand on this debate, Revelation was written by John of Patmos, and this John

1. Bart D. Herman, *Armageddon: What the Bible Really Says About the End* (New York: Simon & Schuster, 2023), 42.

was a real person impacted by the culture and political realities of his lifetime. All evidence points to the understanding that he did, in fact, believe Jesus was going to return very soon within his lifetime. It appears Paul had this belief as well. We cannot be afraid to acknowledge that these biblical writers were wrong, in the most literal sense.

More importantly, John was writing the letters that we now call the Book of Revelation to very real people who lived during a real time and in a real place. Revelation is dated at the end of the first century, just a few decades after the destruction of the Temple. He was writing about 2,000 years ago to seven communities of Jesus followers in western Asia Minor, today known as Türkiye. These seven communities were, from the perspective of John of Patmos, being oppressed under Domitian's rule. These communities had known violence and deep suffering, and they were clinging to the Jesus story and to the belief that in the end, God would make those who were oppressing them pay for their sins. The Revelation of John can be read as a way to provide hope to his seven churches and to convince them to stay faithful and not give in to the ways of the Roman Empire.

He was writing specifically to this audience, using references they would have understood. He was not writing to an audience of twenty-first century Americans living in a democratic and capitalistic society. Revelation is not, however, irrelevant for us today. John was telling these seven churches that the Roman way—the way of violence and war and exploitation and expansion and oppression and control and accumulation of wealth—was on its way to ultimate destruction. Unfortunately, John's own revenge fantasies took over, and Revelation ends up placing Jesus and his followers as the new global power who controls and oppresses and expands its dominion. This is more in line with the Roman way of imperialism than what the New Testament tells us about the teachings of Jesus. For Jesus, the problem was wealth and oppressive power. For John, the problem was who had the wealth and oppressive power. It is up to us to decide who we follow.

When Martin Luther translated the Bible into German during the Protestant Reformation, he demoted Revelation to an appendix. Remember, Martin Luther was a faithful Catholic priest who never intended to begin a new denomination but instead wanted to reform Catholicism. Furthermore, he was a priest and scholar who insisted on the authority of the Bible over church doctrine and tradition, even at the risk of heresy charges and death. Instead of pretending that Revelation should be revered, he put his intellectual pride aside and said that he struggled to see divine meaning in this book and doubted it should be included with the rest of scripture. Christians today continue to disagree about the meaning and importance of the Book of Revelation and the meaning of this apocalyptic text. Nevertheless, we have this text in our Bibles, so the debate continues.

Apostles

Apostle comes from the word *apostolos*, which originally meant "sent one." An apostle is an ambassador or messenger. The good news of Jesus was spread not through political propaganda and announcements, but through unlikely messengers—apostles—often in hushed corners and secret meetings. Messages that contradicted the Roman Empire's power, like those about Jesus, were spread through hidden communication networks of enslaved people, women, day laborers, and other lowly members of Roman society. These messages were generally spoken rather than written. The ambassadors of Jesus engaged in what can be viewed as gossip when spreading the Christian message.

Gossip comes from the word *godsibb*, literally meaning "God relations" and often refers to a godparent or close sibling/kin. In other words, it describes a close spiritual bond. The word *gossip* has a history particularly intertwined with womanhood because women's friends would often become godmothers. This understanding of gossip as unofficial communication between members of marginalized communities helps us make sense of apostles spreading the gospel ("good news"). Women played a significant role in spreading Christianity as they labored alongside one another, supported one another, and shared together in spaces that were largely ignored by men of Roman citizenship. Enslaved people, too, spread messages about Jesus's teachings as they traveled to deliver messages for their enslavers.

When traveling, this unassuming array of apostles often received lodging and food from members of Jesus communities, depending on the recommendations of trusted people within the communities. The gospel of Jesus spread as a message that those with power viewed as a sort of gossip. The spread of the good news began in large part with women, enslaved people, and peasants.

Ascension

When Thutmosis III, ruler of Egypt from around 1479 to 1425 BCE, became Pharaoh, he proclaimed: "The god of heaven is my father. I am his son. He has begotten me, and commanded me to sit on his throne."[2] This statement was responded to with prayers suitable for a god. With each new ruler came promises of salvation sent directly from the heavens; the emperor was seen as the people's savior. Jesus, therefore, was not the first person to be called the Son of God or Savior.

2. Ethelbert Stauffer, *Christ and the Caesars: Historical Sketches* (Eugene, OR: Wipf & Stock, 1952), 37.

We see the similarities in language to describe political rulers and Jesus even more directly when we explore the life of Julius Caesar. The Roman people glorified Julius Caesar following his death, and they sang of him being slain by those he saved, in texts that sound much like those of the Good Friday liturgy. When Julius Caesar died, twelve witnesses said they saw a comet appear in the sky. Augustus, Julius Caesar's son, said that was Julius Caesar ascending to his right place among the gods in heaven. The phrase that became popular was: "I saw the Son of God ascend to the right hand of God the Father."[3] The right hand was a symbol of power in the ancient world. The person sitting to the right of a king, sometimes called the king's "hand" throughout history, was powerful within a kingdom.

The notion that God incarnate dies and ascends did not begin with Jesus. Instead, the language we use to describe Jesus of Nazareth was first used to describe Caesar. The concept of ascending to heaven also appears in the Epic of Gilgamesh, which predates the Bible.

There is further reason to read the powerful story of Jesus's ascension as metaphorical, making it more meaningful than literal language can communicate. Acts 1:1–11, attributed to Luke, states there are forty days between Easter and Ascension Day. Luke 24:1–53, on the other hand, has the Easter and Ascension events occurring on the same day. The same author uses different timelines in these two tellings of the same story, which can support that this is not about a literal telling of time, but instead a symbolic telling of time.

Without understanding this, we lose what Jesus's earliest followers were trying to communicate: that Jesus was anti-empire. Jesus did not only come to say he is God. He also came to tell us that Caesar is not

3. Rob Bell, "Jesus, Domitian and The Book of Revelation," filmed 2018, YouTube video, posted by John JP Patterson, 56:33, May 16, 2018, https://youtu.be/uThyuSy8CsM?si=CiuyJRldyUmGkdrv

God. As Christians, we claim one human as savior, and that is Jesus, who came to denounce power structures and teach us that those in power cannot be the source of our hope.

Brood of Vipers

The phrase brood of vipers," which is used by both John the Baptist and Jesus of Nazareth, has a linguistic harshness that is lost to modern ears. John the Baptist addresses the Pharisees and Sadducees who come to his baptism using this phrase, and Jesus uses this phrase to rebuke the Pharisees and teachers of the law for their hypocrisy.

To modern ears, "brood of vipers" does not hit us as an insult the same way it would have in antiquity. If we take a moment, we see a connection to venomous snakes and perhaps a label pointing to someone's poisonous and dangerous ways.

Understanding that this language used by Jesus borders the profane is important. Without knowing this, we risk softening Jesus's anger. Jesus used intense and harsh language to make his points. Our culture leans towards an understanding of Jesus that is divine in nature. Trinitarian theology does not state Jesus is fifty percent divine and fifty percent human, but instead one hundred percent each. In our own identities, we are not cut into pie slices. I am, at any given moment, completely a mother and a professor and a wife and a writer and a daughter. I am all of these things, always. So, too, was Jesus fully divine and fully human at every moment. In his humanity, he lashed out in righteous anger as many of us do throughout our lives. Understanding the language Jesus used humanizes him in necessary ways.

To use profane language is deeply human. To use this kind of language invokes an emotional part of our humanity. Or perhaps the emotional part of our humanity evokes the use of this kind of language. Either way, it's a human practice that Jesus participated in from time to time.

Second-tier swear words are those that have been watered down to avoid using profanity in conjunction with God and Jesus. For example, *golly*, *gosh*, and *goodness gracious* are all used in place of swearing in the names of God's goodness and grace.

We live in a culture affected by purity expectations, and this includes a preference for language that avoids profanity. Some people have strong opinions about using God-language as profanity, and perhaps rightfully so. However, many Christians are against using profanity at all. No matter the ethical stance we take on profane language, we must be able to reconcile our ethics with the fact that Jesus was known to occasionally use profane language during his human life.

Carpenter

Jesus is referred to directly as a *tekton* in Mark 6:3, which is often translated as a "carpenter." However, Jesus of Nazareth's occupation as a *tekton* (Mark 6:3) could be appropriately translated as a woodworker, builder, bricklayer, stonemason, or carpenter. *Tekton* is the root of the word *architect*. As a *tekton*, or carpenter, Jesus would have been a peasant, ranked just above slaves in the economic system of his day. In fact, tekton is what the Romans used to refer to uneducated peasants—as Jesus likely was. As a carpenter, Jesus would have been smelly, sweaty, and dirty—and especially interesting as he came to be called the Messiah or Christ, meaning the anointed or perfumed one.

Nazareth was a small, rural village in lower Galilee and home to only a small number of Jewish families. The village lacked roads, contained one shared bath of collected rainwater for the entire population, and consisted of illiterate peasants who made a living mostly as farmers and day laborers. Nazarenes, like Jesus and his family, lived in two-room homes, and could not afford to pay for carpentry work. Jesus likely traveled to Galilee's capital city of Sepphoris, a city within walking distance of Nazareth, for work as a carpenter or *tekton*. Sepphoris was a Jewish city, but it was wealthy compared to Nazareth, with two-story homes, large public baths with plenty of water, a Roman theater that could seat over four thousand people, and paved roads everywhere. Jesus likely worked as a day-laborer in Sepphoris six days a week, returning home each night to Nazareth. He would have become familiar with the stark differences between the poor and the wealthy, which might have informed his teachings and preachings.

Christ

Often, we hear Jesus referred to as Jesus Christ. "Christ," of course, is not Jesus's last name. *Christ* is the Greek form of the Hebrew word for *Messiah*. *Messiah* is from the Hebrew word *mashiach*, which means "anointed one." A king was anointed with oil, hence, the anointed one. This Christ identity is connected with the Davidic prophecy, the belief that a descendant of King David would come to reign and bring peace once again.

However, there was no unified understanding of the coming Messiah, or Christ. Some Jews expected a priest, others expected a king, and some expected two Messiahs to fulfill this prophecy. For Christians, Christ became the title given to Jesus. This connection between "Christ" and "anointed one" is often lost today.

How we define Christ has much to do with the Great Schism of 1054, when Christianity split into Western Roman Catholicism and Eastern Orthodoxy. This split between the West (Latin) and East (Greek) caused a stark difference in how we understand Jesus. The West tends to focus on rationality, certainty, and Jesus's humanity and individual nature, while the East is more comfortable embracing the mysterious and cosmic Christ identity. In the West, much of the Christian message has been lost to us because of this schism. The West tends to see Jesus as an individual who rose from the dead, while the East discusses Jesus's resurrection as the corporate salvation of humanity through Christ's destruction of hell.

Christ is not simply a title only given to the historical person of Jesus. Christ is a universal presence in all things. John 1:1 says: "In the beginning was the Word, and the Word was with God, and the Word was God." Here, "Word" is a translation of *Logos*, which means reason or logic. John 1:14 goes on to say, "And the Word became flesh and lived among us," which many interpret as a connection between the Word and Christ.

Paul often discussed Christ as existing in Jesus, but also beyond Jesus. For example, in Galatians 2:20, Paul says: "it is no longer I who live, but it is Christ who lives in me." Similarly, he says in Colossians 1:27: "Christ in you, the hope of glory." Paul is discussing Christ as related to Jesus, but also as more than a historical figure. In 1 Corinthians 12, Paul discusses believers as the body of Christ. This suggests that Christ is an identity.

Christ is not only used to describe the identity of an individual or community, though. Paul also says in 2 Corinthians 5:17: "If anyone is in Christ, there is a new creation." Many interpret this passage as a claim about cosmic renewal. Christ can be understood and experienced as the force or energy behind the reconciliation of all things. Romans 8:18–23 discusses this need for reconciliation in all things.

This view of Christ allows divinity to be seen as accessible and universal. It can break us open to include all things—all people, nonhuman animals, and creation—in our spiritual awareness. Christ is the presence in all things. Jesus the Christ uniquely embodied this Christ presence, but Christ is not limited to Jesus.

Donkey

For Christians, the divine message of anti-violence is especially evident in the life of Jesus. Jesus knowingly rides a donkey into Jerusalem, a dangerous place full of powerful people opposed to his message. Palm branches were waved and laid on the ground as Jesus entered Jerusalem, and the people of the city cheered: *Hosanna! Hosanna!*—meaning "God save us!" Jesus's entrance stood in contrast to the triumphant entrance Romans were used to. He was not coming into the city to claim the empire as his own. Jesus coming into Jerusalem on a donkey was to communicate his purpose.

This is a nod to Zechariah 9:9: "See, your king comes to you; triumphant and victorious is he, humble and riding on a donkey, on a colt, the foal of a donkey." Often, the thinking stops there. Jesus is coming into Jerusalem on a donkey, just as Zechariah says. People expect Jesus to fight and to rule like a king. However, Zechariah 9:10 goes on to say that he will "cut off the chariot from Ephraim and the warhorse from Jerusalem." Chariots and horses are another way to say war, conflict, and violence. Jesus's arrival on a donkey and its connections to Zechariah 9:9 demonstrated a new way, a peaceful way, a way that lacks even a shield. Self-preservation often has to be shed in the peaceful way Jesus taught.

In the Roman Empire, the donkey had many symbolic meanings. Politically, the donkey was used derogatorily to mock political figures, symbolizing stubbornness and stupidity. In Roman and Greek literature, the donkey was sometimes used to convey simplicity or lowliness. This can be seen in writings of Homer, Aesop, and Apuleius. All these symbolic uses affect the way we understand Jesus coming into Jerusalem on a donkey. The Christian story, of course, has infused additional meaning into the image of a donkey.

Jesus's nonviolent arrival does not mean that he was avoiding conflict. Jesus comes into Jerusalem knowing he has spoken out against religious and political powers. Claiming a Messiah identity was punishable as treason, since it was tantamount to declaring war on the empire. Jesus rode into Jerusalem on this physical symbol.

◇◇◇

Eternal Life

Time as we understand and experience it is, in fact, stretchy and flexible rather than static and non-changing. It takes eight minutes and twenty seconds for the light from the sun to reach our planet, meaning when we see the sun shining outside the window, the light is already eight minutes and twenty seconds old. Beyond the sun, our nearest star is Proxima Centauri; light from Proxima Centauri is four years old by the time it arrives to us. Because light takes time to reach us, everything we see is in the past. Time is also relative to our location; a solar day on Earth, the time from one sunrise to the next, is 24 hours (give or take a few minutes) while a solar day on Mercury is 1,408 hours. Distant galaxies appear to be moving faster than nearby galaxies, which suggests the universe is accelerating as it expands. According to the laws of physics, you would age more slowly if you travel extremely fast: flying at ninety-nine percent of the speed of light into the star Sirius would age a traveler less than two and a half years on arrival compared to the seventeen years that would pass on Earth.

If this is too abstract, think of a time when you've lost track of time. Perhaps it was when you were playing with your kids, writing at your desk, crocheting a blanket, or on vacation with loved ones. You weren't watching the clock, and time seemed to expand or perhaps stop. It was as if time did not exist. This was an experience of eternity, and many of us have already known eternal life in this way. Experiencing eternal life is about sinking into an awareness of the present moment and ridding ourselves from distraction—including the distraction of time.

Eternity is not the same thing as forever. Eternity is not time that has no end but rather the lack of time. Eternity is a place that exists outside of linear time as we know it. Eternal life is not life that goes on and on; it is life somewhere beyond the rigid constraints of time. It is a way of living now, and it is a lot more accessible than we think. The observance of Sabbath reminds us to return regularly to the experience of eternal life. As a sanctuary in time rather than space, Sabbath recognizes peace beyond the constraints of time by practicing awareness of the present.

The Gospels tell the story of someone asking Jesus what they must do to have eternal life. They are not asking Jesus about the afterlife, but about how to live a life with full awareness of and connection to God now. Jesus responds to the question by saying they must keep the commandments. This makes sense: we cannot be in the present moment when we are killing or lying or committing adultery. These would be distractions, to say the least. Jesus goes on to tell them to sell their possessions and give their money to the poor, because wealth too is a distraction to living with full awareness of God in the present. The commandment to observe Sabbath was a radical new orientation for the ancient Israelites during their years in the wilderness. In contemporary ancient cultures at the time, people viewed time as cyclical, with nothing new believed to ever happen. The Israelites' embrace of the present moment, following God's commandment, yielded unexpected newness in their experience of time.

When Christianity confines eternal life to the spiritual realm, faith risks becoming overly spiritualized and disconnected from the present experience. Christianity exists in the physical world, too. Eternal life that is rooted in the present moment allows us to experience Christ in the present moment. Christ is always coming, an eternal coming: in this moment, and the next, and the one after that. Here and now. And now. And now. It seems, then, that the only place to be is here and now, fully present in a sanctuary of time.

◇◇◇

Essenes

During Jesus's life, there were several Jewish sects, among them the Pharisees, the Sadducees, the Herodians, the Essenes, and the Zealots. Much of what we know about the Essenes comes from the time after 1947, when the Dead Sea Scrolls were discovered. Scholarly consensus is that these scrolls, found south of Jericho, are remains of an Essene library likely hidden 1900 years ago during a tumultuous time. It is possible that these scrolls were hidden around the time of the destruction of Jerusalem.

In addition to being widely believed to be the authors of the Dead Sea Scrolls, the Essences were Jewish monks who lived separately from society. They had a strong focus on apocalyptic beliefs, so they lived in strict monastic societies, practiced celibacy, and prepared for God's kingdom. The Essenes expected God to intervene and put them in charge of the Temple. Interestingly, the Essenes are not explicitly mentioned in the New Testament, but they were active during this time in history. However, John the Baptist's focus on preparing for God's kingdom and desert lifestyle has led many to believe he was associated with the Essenes.

We often think of Judaism during Jesus's time as having a unified vision and interpretation of the faith, but this is untrue. Like Christianity, there were many variants of Judaism, each with their own sets of beliefs, practices, and political alignment.

Father

Referring to God as Father is a political statement. Julius Caesar was given the title *Pater Patrae* by the Roman Senate, meaning "father of the fatherland."[4] This title was given to rulers that followed Julius Caesar, and eventually this lingo became part of the empire's culture.

The Roman household code was modeled after the Roman political system, and is, in Latin, the *paterfamilias*. The *paterfamilias* placed men at the head of their household, dominating over their wife, children, and enslaved people. We see this cultural code in the letters to the Colos-

4. Amy-Jill Levine, *Sermon on the Mount: A Beginner's Guide to the Kingdom of Heaven* (Nashville: Abingdon Press, 2020), 74.

sians and Ephesians, writings often credited to Paul. This system is not unlike our patriarchal societies today.

The father in this Roman system is seen as the god of his household. The Roman emperor was seen as the father and god of Roman territories. Although emperors were respected as the ultimate paterfamilias of the Roman territories and often revered even beyond their death, this reverence did not always extend beyond their reign. When an emperor died or was overthrown—especially in times of political instability—it was not uncommon for their family to be killed to eliminate rival claims to power. This gave emperors, or the fathers of the empire, reason to work towards control and stability that would outlast their reign.

In this context, we can see what an anti-imperial sentiment it was to call Israel's God "Father." The language of the *paterfamilias* system suggests loyalty to the God of Israel over the emperors and power structures in place. It is a statement about whom Jews and Jesus communities were giving authority.

Furthermore, early Jesus communities often referred to their leaders as "Father," another anti-empire statement. We continue to see priests and pastors in various denominations addressed as Father (or Mother), a practice linguistically rooted in this rebellion against the emperor.

Subculture continues to counter power structures, and language shifts along with culture. Female Episcopal priests are often called Mother. Even in early Jesus communities, we see some communities rejecting the notion that a *paterfamilias* was needed. Chloe led a Jesus community in Corinth. Thecla traveled with Paul as his equal. Many Jesus communities were not led by fathers. And still, to refer to a faith leader as Father is to reject the emperor as Father.

◇◇◇

Feet

We use euphemisms regularly. We say people "slept together" to mean they had sexual relations. The Bible also uses euphemisms. In Hebrew texts, it is often said that two people "knew each other." Additionally, when referencing male sexual organs, biblical texts will instead talk of a man's feet. For an example of this, see Ruth 3:4–14. Ruth's mother-in-law, Naomi, instructs Ruth to wash herself, put on her best clothes, and go to Boaz to uncover his feet and lie down with him. Of course, Ruth is supposed to uncover something besides his feet.

The text goes on to say that Ruth lays at his feet until the morning. Those who read the texts during gatherings in early Jesus communities, a role we would later formalize as the lector, had control over how they read biblical texts and writings about Jesus, and they would adjust the words for the audience as they were reading. For example, if there were children present, the reader would have likely said that two people were lying down together, instead of saying they were having sexual relations. These changes in phrases found their way into later translations of biblical texts.

Of course, this sexual scene takes place before Ruth and Boaz were married. This is interesting because sex before marriage is often touted as unbiblical. However, Ruth and Boaz do eventually get married. Furthermore, Ruth and Boaz's relationship must occur for the familial line of David to go on. As we know, the line of David is part of the messianic prophecy of the Bible that leads to Jesus, since the Bible places Jesus's family in the line of David.

Flood

There are a number of similarities between the Epic of Gilgamesh and the book of Genesis. The earliest Epic of Gilgamesh stories predate the earliest biblical stories by about nine hundred years, and there are many English translations.[5] Despite the difference in dating, we see many commonalities. For example, the Epic of Gilgamesh story features Ut-napishtim and his wife in the garden paradise of Dilmun, and Genesis places Adam and Eve in the garden Eden. There are additional similarities when we consider that the Epic of Gilgamesh has Enkidu made from clay just like Adam in Genesis. In the Epic of Gilgamesh, the goddess Ishtar has a tree of life guarded by a serpent, and Genesis also has a tree and snake.

The Epic of Gilgamesh has a flood story similar to that of Noah. In both stories, a divine decision is made to destroy humanity—God in Genesis acts due to human disobedience, while in the Epic of Gilgamesh, the gods are disturbed by human noise. Each story instructs an individual to build a boat with precise dimensions, sealed with pitch to withstand the flood. Both stories involve gathering many living creatures to preserve life. The duration of the flood differs (forty days and nights in Genesis versus seven days in Gilgamesh) but in both, the boats come to rest on a mountain once the waters recede. Each story involves the sending out of birds to find dry land: a dove and a raven in Genesis; a dove, swallow, and raven in Gilgamesh. After the flood, both Noah and Utnapishtim offer sacrifices to the divine. Each man is rewarded: Noah receives God's covenant and the rainbow as a sign, while Utnapishtim is granted immortality.

There are too many similarities for coincidence, suggesting a common cultural origin. Perhaps the similarities serve to draw attention to where the stories do diverge. The biblical account emphasizes a covenant

5. My favorite English translation of the Epic of Gilgamesh: Stephen Mitchell, trans., *Gilgamesh: A New English Versio*n (New York: Washington Square Press, 2006).

with a single God, while the Mesopotamian story portrays multiple gods acting in more erratic and unpredictable ways. The flood story shows a different kind of divinity: the one God of Israel who is in relationship with people and makes promises in the context of this relationship.

Sumerian culture and biblical culture are separated by a millennium, and yet there is a direct connection between the two: the patriarch Abraham. Genesis 11 seems to rattle off a long list of genealogical facts, and to a reader lacking context this can seem meaningless, but it is important to notice that Abraham, originally named Abram, is from Ur of the Chaldeans. Ur is a Sumerian city, so Genesis shows us a connection between Sumer and Abraham.

It is estimated that Abraham left Sumer around 1900–1800 BCE. Of course, Sumer was conquered—as all civilizations seem to be on a long enough timeline. However, Abraham brought Sumerian remnants with him to Canaan, including stories from the Epic of Gilgamesh. The parallels between the two tales strongly suggest that the Noah story was shaped by earlier Mesopotamian flood myths, adapted to fit the Hebrew worldview. The differences highlight the unique worldview of the Hebrew authors, even as they worked with familiar ancient Near Eastern traditions.

Forty

It rained for forty days and forty nights during the flood. Moses spent forty days and forty nights on Mount Sinai before returning to the Israelites in the desert with God's law. The Israelites wandered the desert for forty years. Spies in Canaan explored the land for forty days before reporting back to Moses and the Israelites. Elijah traveled for forty days and nights to Mount Horeb. Goliath taunted the Israelites for forty days before David defeated him. Jesus fasted for forty days and forty nights in the wilderness when he was tempted by Satan and appeared to his disciples for forty days after his resurrection.

Repeated references to the number forty in the Bible are no coincidence. These stories all have something in common—trial and transformation. Think of a time in your life when you were most changed. Likely, this story contains pain and suffering—a divorce, the loss of a loved one, an illness, a failure, a rejection, or termination from a job. There is rarely transformation without trial.

This use of the number forty to communicate trial and transformation extends beyond the Bible, too. In Islamic tradition, Muhammad was forty years old when he received his first revelation from the angel Jibril (Gabriel), marking the beginning of his prophetic mission. In Sufism, a period of forty days is observed for spiritual retreat and purification. Many Hindu spiritual practices last forty days. The Buddha is said to have meditated under a tree for forty days before reaching enlightenment. In Ancient Greek tradition, Pythagoras and his followers fasted and reflected for forty days.

The symbolic use of forty is everywhere, including in the Christian practice of Lent. Lent is a time of fasting and reflection leading up to Easter, lasting forty days, excluding Sundays.

Forty days is the time between Easter and Ascension Day, which comes from Acts 1:1–11. However, Luke 24:1–53 has all of these Easter and Ascension events occurring on the same day. The same author, in Acts and Luke, tells the same story but with different timelines. Some have argued that this is not about a literal telling of time, but instead a symbolic telling of time.

The word *quarantine* comes from the word *quarantena*, which means "forty days" because people on ships were kept isolated for forty days after arrival to prevent the spread of disease. Quarantine is often thought about in relation to disease, but it also has to do with a journey of isolation. People isolate for many reasons—to avoid spreading contagious illness, to connect with nature and the divine, to attend rehab to get sober, or to give something up for the forty days of Lent. It's an interesting coincidence that pregnancy, the process leading up to literal birth and new life, is also measured on a forty-week timeline.

Gentile

The English word "ethnic" comes from the ancient Greek word *ethnos*, which means "to belong to a people or place." To belong to a group of people in a particular place also meant you worshiped the gods of that particular *ethnos*. As the Roman Empire continued to conquer people and lands, it was expected that people's identities would no longer belong to their previous *ethnos* and gods, but instead to their new god—the emperor. As we know, that's not how ethnic identity works. We all bring with us the traditions and identities of the people and lands we come from.

Ethnos is often translated as "gentile" and is often capitalized as Gentile in the New Testament, specifically in writings credited to Paul. Later, we came to understand Gentile to mean a person who was not a Jew and, ultimately, a person who was a Christian. However, that is not necessarily how the earliest Jesus communities would have understood this. The Greek word *ethnos* in the first two centuries of the common era meant all nations (including Jews), pagan nations, or simply other groups of people. Jewish versus Christian identity was not implied in all uses of this word. In Greek, the word *ethnos* was more neutral and flexible.

Israel was a place to belong. For the first two centuries following the death of Jesus, there was little separation between Jews and Gentiles. Jesus communities acknowledged the God of Israel and the Torah, and they intermingled with Jews. Belonging to a Jesus community also often meant belonging to Israel and Israel's God. Understanding the context of the word "gentile" helps us see that there was not a clear divide between Jews and Jesus followers in the first two centuries following Jesus's death.

◇◇◇

Give to God what is God's

The poor in Galilee were being taxed to the point of struggling to survive while the Romans and the Jewish elite were living lavish lives. Jesus saw commerce taking place at the Temple, and he was enraged. While not illegal, with the Temple and the Romans in cahoots, Jesus's flipping of the tables (Mark 11:15–18 and also in the other three gospels) was the equivalent of treason and a crucifiable offense.

At the time, there was a large, active gang of Jewish bandit revolutionaries working to take back the land from their Roman oppressors. For example, in Matthew 22:22, the Pharisees, likely witnessing Zealot-like behavior, tried to trick Jesus. Jesus was asked: "Is it lawful to pay taxes to the emperor, or not?" Jesus answers by asking them for a denarius, or a coin, and asking whose image is on it. Of course, it is the head of Caesar. He says to give to Caesar what is his and to give to God what is God's. This is not, as public opinion has had us believe for centuries, entirely a verse about caring less about earthly matters like money and more about worshiping God. Instead, there is more going on here.

This story contains evidence of two conflicting groups, the Zealots who rebel against the Roman occupation and the religious elite who benefit from the Roman occupation. This could be interpreted as Jesus admitting to the religious elite and witnesses that he is more aligned with the revolutionaries than those with power. Jesus's answer is more than a statement about taxes; it is also about his stance on the Roman occupation of their land altogether.

Interestingly, this is not the only time in history when the Temple or the Church have been guilty of exploiting believers for the benefit of those in power. Martin Luther was disappointed in the Catholic Church for the same reason Jesus of Nazareth was disappointed in the Temple: taking advantage of the poor. Luther called out his Church for collecting money to save souls in purgatory, all the while the Church was getting richer and the poor among them were being neglected. This behavior continues today. There is reason to be upset with those Christians who collect money from believers so their leaders can buy private jets and lavish vacation homes, all while neglecting the poor among us.

To give to God what is God's is to refuse a system of oppression where the poor are increasingly indebted to the rich and the governmental policies make the rich richer. None of us have a clean dollar in our account, and giving to God what is God's requires us to reconcile our own collaborations with oppressive systems.

God and Our Names for God

The word "God" has been impacted by culture and those in power. Religious language has a long history of adapting to the cultural understandings of various peoples. Christianity began in the Middle East, and it quickly spread into Greek and Latin-speaking communities. To disseminate this story, new language needed to be used. In Greek, the word for God is *Theos*. This is the root for words like theology, meaning the study of God and religion.

Christianity continued to spread, and when it reached Germanic tribes, it was translated once again. In Germanic languages, the Greek *Theos* became God. The Greek for Jesus is *IHSOUS*. Terms used for God came to refer to Jesus. Writers of the New Testament used *Lord* to refer to Jesus in an effort to make connections between the God of the Hebrew Bible and Jesus of Nazareth.

Our understanding of the concept of God is often limited. The word *god* predates Christianity, and has its roots in Germanic words signifying "to pour or offer sacrifice." Anything offered a sacrifice was considered a god. When the Germanic people became Christians, lowercase *god* became capitalized *God*. Germanic languages have gendered words (that is nouns are considered feminine, masculine, and neuter) and God was grammatically neuter. Of course, God eventually became considered masculine because of Christianity's patriarchal history. This emphasis on a masculine God limits our understanding and experience of divinity in dangerous and harmful ways.

To describe or name God, we must stretch our language. We can only describe God with language if we embrace metaphor. Any literal language will fall short. When we say "the Lord is my shepherd," we are using a metaphor. In fact, God is discussed using metaphors throughout the Bible—shepherd, lamb, dove, fire, light, rock, fountain, mother, woman in labor, and many others.

Words like God, Lord, Savior, Son of God, and Father are often used for God. All are inherently political titles. Kings and emperors used these titles for themselves throughout history, pre-dating Jesus and the existence of Christianity.

Ultimately, whatever language we use to name God is an effort to name that which is unnamable. To give something language is to put a box around it, and God is by definition uncontainable. Any time we say

"God," it is an attempt to pin down a butterfly. And once a butterfly is pinned, it is no longer butterfly-ing.

Good and Evil

In the opening chapters of the book of Genesis, we have the infamous tree of knowledge of good and evil. Good and evil in Hebrew are *tob* and *ra*, which can also be translated as pleasure and pain. Eating from this tree results in not knowing pleasure without pain, or pain without pleasure. This makes sense to me. Everything we want is on the other side of something we don't want. This is the reality we find ourselves living in. To gain muscle, we must put in the painful work that is exercise. To get a new job, we must put in the work of gaining the necessary experience or education. To become a good writer, we must put in many years of painfully bad writing. Love itself is simultaneously pleasure and pain. Ask any parent. Pleasure and pain coexist. It's in the design of human maturity.

Gaining the knowledge of good and evil, or pain and pleasure, can be interpreted as the process of growing up and maturing. Realizing that everything good also has a shadow side is part of maturing. This dualistic categorization of the world into good and evil is likely an influence from the time when Jews lived under Persian rule, from about 539–332 BCE. Zoroastrianism emphasizes good versus evil.

In fact, evil has not always been understood as a single force aligned against goodness and God. It used to be seen as coming from many sources. Between Second Temple Judaism and early Christianity, the idea developed that there was one evil force opposed to God. The Hebrew word *hasatan*, or the accuser, shifted to refer to the evil one, and many other names have been given to this accuser, including serpent, devil, and Satan.

Concepts of good and evil have been a topic of debate among philosophers and theologians for a long time. Incorporating the linguistic context can help us nuance this debate even further. Perhaps good and evil are not tidy categories that we can neatly separate. Like the pleasure and pain that often accompany each other, good and evil may come from the same tree.

Gospel

"Gospel" and "good news" both come from the same Greek word *evangelion*, which can also be translated as "announcement," and from the Old English word *godspel*, meaning "good news." An evangelist is the title given to those who wrote the gospels, and it means the "good-news giver." The Greek prefix *eu-* means "good" and becomes the Latin prefix *ev-*, while the Greek root *angel-* becomes the Latin *angel-*. *Angelos* and *angelus*, which come from the same root as the English word *angel*, mean messenger. Therefore, the Greek word *evangelion* means "good message."

Evangelion has its roots in the Roman Empire. Before the gospels existed, there were government announcements offering good news for the citizens of the Roman Empire, which were referred to as *evangelion*. Typically, these political gospel announcements would be about something like the emperor's birthday. Good news is a political phrase originating with Gaius Octavian, Rome's first emperor. He ended a civil war by conquering Mark Antony and Cleopatra, and was given the title Augustus, meaning "exalted one." Additionally, ancient inscriptions identify Augustus's birth as the beginning of the gospel, or good news, of his kingdom. Therefore, later emperor's birthdays continued to be seen as announcements of good news, which is in line with how future generations came to view Jesus's birth.

The writings that have come to be known as the gospels were named after these Roman announcements of good news, which is a direct statement against the Roman Empire. It is saying: there is good news, and it doesn't come from the victories of the Romans; it comes from the victory of Jesus on the cross.

Harvest

Harvest is an important time. The books of Exodus and Leviticus in the Hebrew Bible contain agricultural rules and structure for the Israelites to use when arranging their shared lives together after liberation. Exodus 23 states that the first fruits of the harvest should be brought to God, meaning it was taken to the Temple, blessed, and given to the clergy and people in need. This is similar to the practice of tithing today: people give a portion of their resources to the church to sustain the clergy, who provide their services to the community and to those in need. Similarly, Leviticus 19 instructs God's people not to reap the edges of their fields and to instead leave parts of the harvest for the poor and the foreigner. Baked into society's structure was caring for the earth, the poor, and foreigners. This was believed to be the way the kingdom of God was structured.

The agricultural cycle was deeply embedded in the lives and social structure of the Israelites. There was a time to labor but there was also a time to pause and celebrate a good harvest. Sometimes the Bible uses the harvest as a metaphor to reveal greater spiritual wisdom. Using the harvest as a metaphor is connected to concepts of time, often symbolizing rhythms of life and divine timing. The harvest is about planting, growing, waiting, and reaping. Ecclesiastes 3 uses this metaphor when stating that there is a time to plant and there is a time to pluck. Just as the harvest is all about seasonal timing, our lives are also about seasons and timing. There is a time to work, a time to rest, a time to wait, a time to act, a time to mourn, and a time to celebrate.

Jesus also referred to the harvest to make his points. For example, in Matthew 9:37, Jesus says that the harvest is plentiful, but there are only a few laborers. He is pointing to the kingdom of God on earth being ripe and ready when he refers to the harvest being plentiful. He is using the harvest to point to the fact that the time was right for the Jewish people to experience the kingdom of God, meaning to live in this God-given way, but there were few willing to resist the Roman occupation. The Romans had corrupted too much of the Jewish community to make the kingdom of God a reality.

The harvest is also used to represent a time of justice. In Greek, the word often translated as "judgment" is *krisis*. While *krisis* can be defined as a sort of decision made about what is right and wrong, it is also defined as "a separation," or "a trial." This makes sense considering a sin is anything that separates us from God and our neighbor.

Jesus's teachings were about timing. He was trying to communicate to his followers that the time for the kingdom was now. This is made especially clear in John 4:35 when he tells his followers to look around at the harvest, which is ripe for harvesting. Again, we see him pleading, using the harvest as a metaphor for divine timing, asking those around him to open their eyes and see the signs of the kingdom of God in the present moment.

He

THERE IS A LOT TO SAY about the short word *he*. Christian doctrine views God as genderless, and yet we refer frequently to God as He, often with that capital "H." Christianity claims a triune God—Father, Son, Holy Spirit. Another way to say this is God the Creator, Jesus, and Spirit. Trinitarian doctrine states that all of these divine identities are one. Jesus, of course, was a historical man. While we often refer to the first person of the Trinity as "He," Spirit has deeply feminine linguistic roots.

Unlike English, many languages are gendered. In linguistics, a grammatical gender system is a specific form of a noun class system, where nouns are assigned to gender categories—the reason why "cat" requires the masculine form of the article in French and Spanish. The Hebrew word for Spirit is *ruach*, and in Greek is *pneuma*. *Ruach* is feminine and *pneuma* is neuter. Jesus spoke Aramaic, in which *rucha* is feminine. The words for Spirit in Greek, Hebrew, and Latin mean "breath," something life-giving and unseen.

Our culture tends to turn gender into a strict binary, when feminine and masculine traits exist in us all to varying degrees. How could God be an exception to this? The Bible supports this. Yes, God is described using masculine imagery—king, father, son, etc. However, the Bible also uses feminine imagery to describe God—mother eagle (Deuteronomy), a mother who has given birth (Deuteronomy), as having a womb and giving birth (Job), midwife (Psalms), a pregnant woman in labor (Isaiah), a nursing mother (Isaiah), among others.

Throughout history, theologians have referred to God using feminine language. Saint Augustine (354–430 CE) described God as a mother, and ancient Armenian church father Gregory of Narek (c.950–c.1005) referred to God as "Mother of All." Julian of Norwich (1342–c.1416) referred to God as Mother. Referring to God using only the male pronoun limits our understanding of God. When I incorporate feminine and masculine traits into my understandings and experiences of God, God becomes more full and authentic in my life.

To discuss the language and concepts behind what it means socially to be considered a man or a woman, we first must understand that masculinity and femininity are concepts controlled by society. In Roman culture, social status for men was gained by being a violent warrior with sexual dominion over women, so bodies with testosterone were hormonally motivated to mold into this image. In Western culture today, social status is given to those with economic achievement.

The Latin word *vir* means "man." *Vir* referred to only a very specific category of human: an adult male who was a Roman citizen, married to a woman, not enslaved, and participated in military activity. To be a *vir*, or man, had less to do with biological sex and more to do with social status and power, found through citizenship, marriage, and military. Not all males were considered men, and not all men were guaranteed to keep this social status. Above all else, men had to display constant courage to keep their manly status.

The scholar Virginia Burrus has researched how gender plays a role in many martyrs' stories, and how early Jesus communities often complicated and rejected gender norms. Traditionally, to be a martyr was seen as the ultimate statement of courage and manliness. Burrus, however, examines the stories of religious martyrs to show how these narratives intentionally flip the narrative that to be a courageous martyr is always linked to manhood. For example, 4 Maccabees tells the story of Antiochus IV Epiphanes forcing Eleazar to eat food forbidden in Jewish tradition. Eleazar, a Jewish man, refused. More interesting than his loyalty to his faith is the way the storyteller focuses on Eleazar's old age. The text makes it clear again and again that he is an old man with gray hairs, and furthermore connects his age to his courage. Antiochus tortures and kills Eleazar. The narrator is making the point that courage does not belong only to the *vir*. It belongs to other categories as well, such as the elderly.

This same text, 4 Maccabees, also discusses the martyrdom of a mother of seven children. Her children die at the hands of Antiochus, and she throws herself into the fire before Antiochus can defile her body. Here, a woman is courageous, in control, and a martyr.

We see the connection between courage and maleness clearly in the *Passion of Perpetua and Felicitas*, one of the earliest Christian texts we have, written by Tertullian of Carthage (in modern-day Tunisia). This text contains the vision of Perpetua fighting an Egyptian gladiator. In this vision, she becomes a man: *facta sum masculus* (I become male). However, the Latin has a play on words. *Facta* is a term of feminine identity, while *masculus* means male. In this statement, she is describing herself as both female and male.

People continue to be uncomfortable with deviations from the gender binary of male-female, yet the kind of gender fluidity we see in martyr narratives is evidence that these realities are not new. Many people point to the Bible for evidence that women cannot be leaders, however, that same Bible provides evidence that women were, in fact, in leadership roles. In Romans 16, Paul lists many female leaders, naming eight of them. In Philippians 4, Paul describes women as his coworkers.

Some women in leadership roles have been erased altogether. For example, Romans 16:7 originally names *Junia*, a woman's name, as one of Paul's apostles. Later biblical manuscripts and translations changed this name into *Junias*, a male name. The intentional erasing and minimizing of women has deep historical roots; however, we cannot deny the importance of women in Jesus's life, beginning with the mothers and grandmothers of his lineage.

The Gospel of Matthew begins with a long list of Jesus's genealogy—forty-two generations to be exact. Typically, lineage is passed down through the males of the family, so it is particularly unusual that this list contains five women—Tamar, Rahab, Ruth, Bathsheba, and Mary. Bathsheba, with whom King David had an affair, is listed as the wife of Uriah, but nonetheless she is listed, unusual as that may be. Listing women in a familial line was unnecessary in the context of genealogical conventions of the time, but this gospel writer includes these five women, which means their stories must be vital to the identity of Jesus.

We cannot discuss *he* without bringing up *they*. It's important to note that *they* as a singular pronoun is acceptable in English. Only a few centuries ago, *you* was a plural word and *thou* was the singular form (as in "thou shalt not kill"). Eventually, *thou* went away and *you* took its place. The singular *they* is already used regularly, for example: somebody left their phone in my car. Other cultures do not have binary female-male gender norms. The Buginese people of Indonesia have five genders and the Native American Zuni tribe has a third gender.

There is a long history of women challenging dominant doctrine and theological assumptions. To challenge dominant notions of gender, we are challenging dominant notions of power, something Jesus taught his followers to do two thousand years ago.

Hebrews

JEWISH HISTORY IS ANCIENT AND COMPLEX. Students of that history quickly notice that the Jewish people are referred to using multiple titles, including Hebrews, Israelites, and Jews. These titles are often used interchangeably, but the shifts in use have everything to do with power and timing.

One of the earliest names used for this community of people was Hebrews. This title was used before the kingdom of Israel was established, and the roots of this term continue to be debated. The word *Hebrews* is related to the Hebrew word *avar*, meaning "to cross over" or "to pass through." Some have argued that this could be a reference to a geographical crossing of rivers or lands. It could also be a reference to being migrants and culturally crossing into new terrain. Either way, the term *Hebrew* is seen by many as a reference to travel and movement, which is a large part of the Hebrew experience throughout history. A debated connection to the word *Hebrew* is the group called the *Habiru* (or *Apiru*) in ancient Near Eastern texts, a loosely organized group of stateless and often marginalized people. Biblically, Abraham is called "Abram the Hebrew," as seen in Genesis 14:13, suggesting that Hebrew originally referred to a particular tribe of wanderers.

When the Hebrew Bible was translated into Greek, the word for Hebrew was adjusted for Greek phonetics. In Latin, the word was kept close to its Greek form as *Hebraeus*, as seen in the Jerome's fourth-century Vulgate. In Greek and Latin, *Hebraeus* started to refer not just to ethnic descendants of Abraham, but also more broadly to Jewish identity. This became especially true when Christianity emerged and needed to distinguish between Jews, Christians, and Gentiles. From Latin, it entered Old French and Middle English as *Ebreu* or *Ebrewe*, eventually becoming *Hebrew* in modern English.

Later, the Hebrews came to be known as the Israelites. This title comes from Jacob, who was given the name Israel, meaning "struggle with God," after he wrestled with an angel of God (Genesis 32:28). Jacob's twelve sons formed the twelve tribes of Israel and the nation of Israel under King Saul, King David, and King Solomon.

◇◇◇

Hell

There are many words in the Bible that have been translated or understood as *hell*, and these words deserve context. The Hebrew writers were not overly concerned with what happens to each individual when they died. In fact, the words *life* and *death* were not always used literally in Hebrew culture. For example, in Deuteronomy 30 when Moses tells the Hebrews to choose life rather than death, this is not about choosing not to die a literal death. In Hebrew consciousness, God was a God of the living. Life is about being connected to God, while death is used to describe a way of life that is disconnected from God. When the afterlife is discussed, various words are used. *Sheol* is used in the Hebrew Bible to refer to the place everybody, good or bad, goes when they die. The idea of an eternal place of punishment had not yet been developed. Some have surmised that *sheol* could be translated as *grave*, although Hebrew had another noun used for this word, because everybody goes to the grave.

In the New Testament, especially in Revelation, *Hades* is used. Hades comes out of the Greek literature, often discussed as a place where we go when we die to rest. In fact, biblical translations like the New Revised Standard Version and English Standard Version capitalize the words *Death* and *Hades* in Revelation to make the point that John is personifying these concepts.

Another word often used in the New Testament that has become associated with hell is the Greek word *Gehenna*. *Ge* means valley, and *henna* means Hinnom. The Valley of Hinnom is a place of torment (Matthew 5:22, 29; 23:15; Mark 9:43–47; Luke 12:5). However, rather than a place of eternal torment after death, it refers to a real place of torment here on earth. In the Hebrew Bible, Gehenna was an actual valley where Canaanites sacrificed children to the god Moloch using fire.[6]

6. Thomas Cahill, *Desire of the Everlasting Hills: The World Before and After Jesus* (New York: Nan A. Talese / Anchor Books, 1999), 80.

In Jesus's time, Gehenna was a fiery pit where people threw their trash, and dogs fought over the garbage with gnashing teeth. The New Testament expands on this literal place to create an image of wickedness, evil, and death.

The notion of hell as a fiery place of torment where we are sent after death to be punished forever is a post-biblical concept. It comes from works like the second century Apocalypse of Peter, fourth century Apocalypse of Paul, medieval art, and Dante's *Inferno*.

Helper

PATRIARCHY HAS DOMINATED SOCIETY FOR MILLENNIA, and biblical translations and interpretations are no exception. For example, Eve is said to be Adam's helper. The word *helper* in Genesis 2 means a helper across from, not beneath or unequal to. There is no inherent hierarchy in the original Hebrew. In the earliest version of Genesis in English poetry (around the eighth century), the word used to describe Eve's role was *fultum*.[7] *Fultum* means help and support, but it also means armed reinforcements and military support. Medieval and Renaissance translators decided on "helper," which I think is lacking a certain oomph.

The Hebrew word *ezer kenegdo* in Genesis is often translated into English as "helper" or "suitable helper." We often presume that Eve's role as a helper places her below Adam in a hierarchy; however, versions of this Hebrew word is used elsewhere in the Bible to describe God's role in man's life. God is a helper of man. For example, Psalm 121:1–2

7. Jenni Nuttall, *Mother Tongue: The Surprising History of Women's Words*. (London: Penguin Random House, 2023), 245.

discusses help that comes from the Lord, but God is not seen as secondary in this instance.

Some rabbinical discourse has interpreted *ezer* to mean "helper" and *kenegdo* to mean "opposite." They have made the point that if a man is not worthy, his wife will oppose him rather than help him. This discourse can contribute to morals concerning mutual respect in relationships, while countering blind obedience in any form of commitment.

Additionally, when Genesis states that God made a woman, the Hebrew word means "built." The woman is the only creature described as being built. The word often translated in English as rib actually means "side" in Hebrew. These are subtle differences, but they result in very different interpretations and understandings.

This pigeonholing of what it means to be a woman has left women out of the dominant Christian narrative. For example, we often hear of only male disciples. Luke 10:1 tells readers of seventy-two disciples, many of whom were women, some discussed by name in the New Testament: Joanna, Mary the mother of James and Joseph, Mary the wife of Clopas, Susanna, Salome, and of course, Mary Magdalene. We continue to see women being forced into secondary and submissive roles in our narratives and our realities.

The fact that so many women have to be reminded of their supposed submissive role regularly speaks more to control, dominance, and indoctrination efforts than it does actual God-given identities. I find it especially interesting that we are reminded that the Genesis story has woman being created from man's rib, considering that men are all born from women's wombs.

Herodians

During Jesus's life, there were several Jewish sects, among them the Pharisees, the Sadducees, the Herodians, the Essenes, and the Zealots. The Israelites were under Roman occupation during Jesus's time, and the Romans did not want constant conflict and violence with the Israelites. To keep the peace while maintaining control, the Romans thought it best to put a Jew in charge of the Jews. This ruling line of Jews were known as the Herodians, or the Herods. The Herodians were more political than religious. They benefited from the Roman system, supported Roman authorities, and helped the Romans tax the public.

King Herod the Great, who was appointed King of Judea by the Romans and ruled from 37 to 4 BCE, was the origin of the Herodian dynasty. His loyalties were split between the Romans and the Jews, evidenced by his projects to expand the Second Temple while simultaneously working to maintain Roman favor.

Herodians were not descendants of the Herod family, but instead supporters of the dynasty that continued to be active during Jesus's lifetime and during the reign of Herod's son, Herod Antipas. Mark 3:6 and 12:13 discuss the Herodians as allies of the Pharisees. They were likely supporters of the Romans who gave their dynasty power, so they were aligned against Jesus for his critique of the political and religious leaders of his day.

We often think of Judaism during Jesus's time as having a unified vision and interpretation of the faith, but this is not correct. Like Christianity, there were many variants of Judaism, each with their own sets of beliefs, practices, and political alignments.

Horse and Chariot

Horses had a very different cultural role in the time of many biblical writings compared to the roles they play in contemporary Western society. The societies in which the most ancient of these texts were created were not fully agrarian, meaning agriculture and farming was not at the center of their economies and cultures. Horses were not used for agricultural labor or transportation but as an important military tool of war. Chariots also were military tools, similar to tanks today.

In Exodus, the sea is parted so that Israelites seeking their freedom from Pharaoh and the Egyptians could escape. When the Pharaoh's horses and chariots attempted to cross the parted sea, the water collapsed in on them and destroyed them all. The imagery of the water being brought down on the horses and chariots can be misconstrued if we don't recognize these things for what they were: weapons of war. As the water sweeps back over the Egyptian horses and chariots, God is destroying weapons of war and those using them from a position of power.

Psalm 20 tells us that some trust in chariots and horses, but others trust in God. A modern translation might read: Some trust in the military, but others trust in God. The United States has a military like never seen before in the history of this planet. We are the only country to ever drop an atomic bomb—and we dropped two! Christian citizens of the United States must be careful when interpreting texts about horses and chariots that we do not become the ones who trust in the military over God.

Interestingly, Deuteronomy 17:16 prohibits horses in Israel. Of course, King Solomon and later kings did not obey. Later, Hebrew prophet Isaiah states (Isaiah 2:7) that the land was filled with horses and chariots. Like Jesus refusing to fight violence with violence, God is calling on Israel to refuse war. Reading biblical texts about horses and chariots can be problematic for those of us who live in a country with an ever-expanding military complex, a country with "In God We Trust" printed on the very money spent on modern-day horses and chariots.

Hosanna

The seventh chapter of John's gospel is about the Festival of Tabernacles, one of the major Hebrew feasts. All seven of these major festivals are listed in the twenty-third chapter of Leviticus. Festivals were arranged around agriculture and seasons. Thousands of people would gather for eight days during the Festival of Tabernacles, the final feast before winter. During this time, they would remember how their God took care of them in the wilderness by providing daily bread (see Exodus for this story), and they would pray for God to provide rain for their crops to thrive come spring. There were no grocery stores or processed food, so little or no rain became a question of survival. On the eighth and final day of this festival, the high priest would pour water and wine together and the thousands of gathered people would chant: *Hosanna! Hosanna!*

Hosanna comes from the Hebrew word *hoshi'ah na'—hoshi'ah* meaning "save" or "deliver," and *na'* meaning an urgent plea. Vital to understanding the origins of this word is this sense of urgency in the word *Hosanna.* These were people who were begging for rain to save them from drought and famine. Human beings love to pretend like we are in control, but the Israelites understood that getting enough rain for crops to thrive was out of their control.

This focus on daily bread with the image of wine and water being poured together is an image of Communion. In liturgical churches, the Eucharistic or Communion prayer includes this nod to scriptural language: "Holy, holy, holy Lord, God of power and might, Heaven and earth are full of your glory. Hosanna in the highest. Blessed is he who comes in the name of the Lord. Hosanna in the highest." As seen in Matthew 21:9, Mark 11:9–10, and John 12:13, the crowds cry out "Hosanna! Hosanna!" when Jesus enters Jerusalem after the Last Supper, or sharing of bread and wine, and before his crucifixion.

As words always do on a long enough timeline, the meaning of *Hosanna* expanded to include more connotations. *Hosanna* later began to have political meaning when the Jewish people were begging to be saved from the Romans who had claimed dominion over their home. Additionally, when Jesus rode on a donkey into Jerusalem, people cheered: *Hosanna! Hosanna!*

We say "Hosanna," or "God save us now," in the celebration of the Eucharist or Communion because Communion is about God right now. Sometimes, people say they "take Communion." However, linguistically and theologically this is incorrect. Communion is not taken. It is received. It is participated in. But it is never taken. It is not something we do, but instead something we are a part of. We are entering into a meal with the divine, in the present moment. It is to be experienced in the present moment. Like thousands of years ago, we, too, gather and cry out "Hosanna! Hosanna!" or "God save us now!"

Jesus's name is even connected to *hosanna*.[8] Jesus is a version of the name Joshua, which is *Yehoshua* in Hebrew, and is related to the Hebrew word for Hosanna, *hoshi'ah na'*. Jesus's entire identity is connected to the idea of salvation.

8. Amy-Jill Levine and Marc Zvi Brettler, *The Bible With and Without Jesus: How Jews and Christians Read the Same Stories Differently* (New York: HarperOne, 2023), 258.

Inn

We read the Christmas story with many Western assumptions. We picture Mary and Joseph being denied a room at the inn, but the word has a very different meaning in the nativity story. The Greek word for inn, *pandocheion*, used in the parable of the Good Samaritan, is not the word used in the Gospel of Luke to describe where Mary gives birth to Jesus. Instead, the word *kataluma* is used, meaning a room in a private dwelling. *Kataluma* is the same word used in Luke 22:11 to describe the upper room where Jesus and his disciples ate the Last Supper. Mary probably gave birth in the home of a family member, in a room typically used for domestic cattle. Rather than being denied a room in an inn as we often think of an inn, it is more likely they were denied a room in personal living quarters.

In Middle Eastern culture, hospitality is sacred. Mary and Joseph being turned away from a public business seems harsh enough, but being denied space in a relative or close friend's home suggests that they could have been unwelcome because of shame and rejection of their unwed and pregnant state. This means the stable was more likely to have been in the lower level of a home where animals were kept, rather than behind an inn. This fits with Luke's narrative inclusion of the manger, or feeding trough.

This has implications for our rhetoric surrounding the Christmas story. It is easy for us to distance ourselves from the idea that a business owner denied a young pregnant woman a room at their establishment, especially as Christians who believe that woman was carrying God incarnate. However, this linguistic nuance complicates our sense of self-righteousness. How many of us would invite someone into our own personal home or space to give birth? Further, who among us would welcome into our home to give birth one who was morally misaligned from what we believed to be righteous? Mary was a young, unwed, pregnant woman. These were reasons enough for her to be rejected in this culture. The Christian story repeatedly provides evidence that God works on the margins, through the rejected and excluded. This is true of Jesus's birth, which foreshadows Jesus's ministry.

Israelites (See Jews)

Jehovah

The Exodus story begins with Moses, and his experiences hearing the one God speaking to him from the burning bush (Exodus 3:1–22) was the beginning of monotheism, a belief in a single God, as we know it today. However, this God needed a name for Moses to tell the Israelites of this God.

God tells Moses that God's name is *YHWH*. Ancient Hebrew was written without vowels, so when we try to pronounce *YHWH* we find ourselves breathing in and out, making the sound of breath. Many scholars, pastors, and believers make connections between this name for God and the breath of life. *YHWH* was considered too sacred to say out loud, so the Jewish people did not say it or even write it. In many versions of the Bible, LORD is written in all caps in place of *YHWH*. Instead of saying the sacred name of *YHWH*, many said *Adonai*, which means "the Lord." Some Jews refused to even say *Adonai*, instead saying *ha-Shem*, meaning "the Name."

Many English speakers pronounce *YHWH* as "Yahweh." Sometimes it is pronounced or written as *Jehovah*. Medieval Christian scholars misunderstood the signal not to pronounce the name of God, and they transliterated it into Latin as Jehovah: "Y" became "J" (common in Latin and early English) and "W" became "V." The Hebrew *YHWH*, plus the vowels from *Adonai*, became "Jehovah." What we do know about the sacred name *YHWH* is that it is in the verb form "to be." Therefore, God told Moses that God is a verb rather than a noun.

Jews

The Israelites, among other groups, colonized Canaan. Under Saul and David's rule, the Israelites were generally united. After King Solomon (970 to 931 BCE), Israel split into two under the rule of his son, Rehoboam: the northern kingdom of Israel and the southern kingdom of Judah. The northern kingdom of Israel was destroyed by the Assyrians and the area became populated by Samaritans. The southern kingdom of Judah was exiled to Babylon around 600 BCE and returned to their country with the Edict of Cyrus in 538 BCE. The Roman province of Judea became known as Palestine after the second century CE Bar Kokhba revolt. During the Hellenistic period, the Greeks referred to the broader region historically associated with Israel and Judah as Palestine. Within this broader territory, the area where a Jewish population remained was known as Judea.

Judah is where we get the title Jew. Initially, the word was used to refer to people from the southern kingdom of Judah, but eventually it was used to refer to all Israelites. Understanding the titles of *Hebrew, Israelites*, and *Jews* is relevant when we discuss who has power. These titles, although often used interchangeably, have distinct historical contexts rooted in land and conflict.

Jubilee

Leviticus discusses a Jubilee. Jubilee is connected to the Sabbath day. On the seventh day, humans rest to experience their liberation. The first eleven verses of Leviticus 25 discuss the sabbatical year. In the seventh year, the land must rest. Fields cannot be sowed, vineyards cannot be pruned, and harvests cannot be reaped. After seven cycles of sabbatical years, there is a Jubilee year.

The next verses of Leviticus 25 discuss the year of Jubilee, which is a year of rest for the land and a time for social renewal. In Jewish history, the Jubilee year is a special year every fifty years focused on renewal and restoration. Jubilee has an interesting linguistic origin. It comes from the Hebrew word *yōbēl*, meaning "ram's horn," which is what was used to sound the start of the Jubilee year on the Day of Atonement. In Latin, *iubilare* means "to shout for joy," and this word influenced the Old French word *jubilé* which became the English word jubilee.

The Jubilee year is a time to shout for joy. It was discussed as a regularly scheduled time in every generation for joy and celebration. Every fiftieth year, there were three major practices associated with this joy and celebration: 1) debts were forgiven, 2) enslaved people were freed, and 3) land was returned to its original owners. This was a year designed to specifically address economic disparities and promote a sense of social justice for each generation in ancient Israel.

Jubilee laws stating that debts were to be forgiven every fifty years freed people from financial bondage. This is especially interesting when we consider that in discussions of debt, we continue to use words like grace and forgiveness, which are words often heard in Christian and religious contexts. For example, the cancellation of debts, a rare occurrence in a capitalistic system focused on profit often earned through the collection of interest on loans, is often called loan forgiveness. Similarly, a bill paid a few days late is often forgiven if paid within a grace period. We have remnants of Jubilee language in our current systems, but still we fall short of the radical and regularly scheduled Jubilee practices described in the Bible. People in power who claim to have a faith rooted in the Bible conveniently forget these biblical texts about the forgiveness of debts. Furthermore, various Bible passages including Leviticus 25:36–37, Exodus 22:25, and Deuteronomy 23:19 prohibit the charging of interest to those within your community who are in need. The Bible is full of economic teachings that favor and protect the poor from exploitation.

Many Christians today say the Lord's Prayer, which can be found in Matthew 6:9–13 and Luke 11:4. Many say ". . . forgive us our trespasses, as we forgive those who trespass against us." However, in the original Greek of Matthew 6:12, the word used is *opheilēmata*, which translates to debts, meaning a financial or moral obligation. In other words, the original Greek of Matthew is about the forgiveness of debts rather than the forgiveness of trespasses. Similarly, Luke 11:4 uses the word meaning sins. While the original Greek of Matthew uses the word *debts*, Luke uses the word *sins*. This word choice makes sense, considering the Gospel of Matthew was written to a Jewish audience who would have been familiar with the laws of Jubilee. The Gospel of Luke, on the other hand, was written to a non-Jewish audience.

The English translation of *opheilēmata* as "trespasses" comes from the fourteenth-century Wycliffe Bible and the sixteenth-century Book of Common Prayer. The word *trespasses*, as opposed to *debts* or *sins*, became common in liturgical settings, and has therefore stuck in many Christian traditions. Nevertheless, an examination of the original Greek of Matthew suggests that a more accurate translation of the Lord's Prayer would mention the forgiveness of debts in alignment with laws of Jubilee.

Freeing enslaved people every fiftieth year was also a large part of Jubilee practices. There is no justifying the horrors of enslavement; however, seeing enslavement in its historical context is necessary to understand many biblical themes. In ancient times, there was not a welfare system in place for those for whom society failed to provide. Instead, people who went unhoused and hungry became enslaved. For many throughout history, enslavement was an excuse to exploit and abuse people without limitations. However, the Israelites were instructed by God to do things differently. They put restrictions on enslavement, which was radical in the ancient context. When the Bible discusses enslavement, it is often connected to the limitations of enslavers and focuses on the freedoms of the enslaved. For example, Exodus 21 states that enslavement cannot last longer than six years unless the enslaved person chooses to remain, and it provides rules about selling daughters and ensures they were treated as wives rather than property.

In the modern sense, the release of enslaved people does not explicitly refer to the release of prisoners. However, enslavement was directly connected to imprisonment and debt in the ancient world. Many people were enslaved or imprisoned because of debt they were unable to pay back. The Jubilee required the cancellation of debts, so by extension, it also required releasing people who were enslaved or imprisoned for financial reasons. Ridding the enslaved and imprisoned of their debts allowed for them to begin fresh.

There is a strong connection between imprisonment and low socioeconomic status. People living in poverty with fewer economic opportunities, higher debt, and unstable housing are significantly more likely to be incarcerated. Policies disproportionately criminalize behaviors associated with poverty and criminalize the use of drugs, which disproportionately affects low-income communities and contributes to high incarceration rates. Finances and debt are inextricably linked to incarceration, so a regular practice of Jubilee addresses both debt and incarceration. Furthermore, a previously incarcerated person in modern society faces barriers due to their criminal record, even for minor offenses. These barriers make it difficult for them to find employment, which contributes to cycles of poverty and results in recidivism and lives hindered by debt. Jubilee practices were created with a sense of wisdom about the connections between debt and enslavement.

One way a person could be freed from enslavement before the Jubilee year was if a male relative bought them out of enslavement. This relative was considered a *go'el*, or redeemer.[9] This is where the meaning of redemption took hold. Redemption was not an unseen spiritual reality, but instead was baked into the social and political policies of ancient Israel. Instead of hoping a redeemer would show up to liberate enslaved Israelites, the Jubilee was a concrete form of redemption observed regularly so all enslavement had an end date.

Of course, for Christians, Jesus the Christ is seen as the ultimate redeemer and Jubilee. Jesus's entire ministry was about freeing captives from whatever bound them. Often, it was the political rulers of the day who were oppressing the people Jesus was determined to liberate.

In addition to forgiving debt and freeing the enslaved, land was also returned to its original owners. Every fiftieth year, ancestral land that was sold was to be returned to its original family. When the Israelites came to Cannan, the land was divided and each family was given a plot. In the ancient world, land was passed down throughout generations of

9. John Bergsma, *Jesus and the Jubilee: The Biblical Roots of the Year of God's Favor* (Steubenville, OH: Emmaus Road Publishing, 2025), 52.

families, and family land was used for many purposes. Ancestors were buried on family land. Food to feed the family was grown on the land. Ancient Israelites often sold their land when they found themselves in a difficult financial situation. When things were desperate, they would sell themselves into enslavement, too. And yet, the Jubilee ensured that this was set right every generation. Having a nation of Israelites without their own land would have brought the Israelites full circle into enslavement again, negating the liberation of the Exodus.

The concept of a Jubilee year can be found beyond Leviticus. For example, Isaiah 61 discusses the "year of the LORD'S favor," referring to the Jubilee year. Isaiah 61 doubles down on themes of Jubilee by mentioning good news for the oppressed, liberty for captives, and release of prisoners. Interestingly, Jesus references this passage in Luke 4:18–19 when he says that he is here to proclaim the "year of the Lord's favor"—referring to the Jubilee year—by bringing good news to the poor and releasing the captives. Jubilee is about forgiving debts, freeing the unfree, and returning land. It is a specific way to arrange political and economic systems.

King James Version

In 1522, William Tyndale, an English scholar during the Protestant Reformation, began to translate the Bible into English from Luther's German translation, the Latin Vulgate, and Erasmus's Greek translation. Tyndale did not translate the Bible into English in its entirety. Myles Coverdale, an English preacher and translator, had that honor. Coverdale did not know Hebrew, so he used the English and German translations to help him complete the first full English translation of the Bible in 1535. Following Tyndale's and Coverdale's work, multiple English versions came onto the scene, including the Geneva Bible in 1560 and the Bishops' Bible in 1568.

There was a desire to unify these multiple English language versions by creating one English Bible with ultimate authority. This was the genesis of the King James Version (KJV). The King James Version was heavily influenced by—and in many ways straight-up plagiarized—Tyndale's work.

The King James Version was created for both religious and political purposes. The Protestant Reformation, which was also taking place in England, was a precursor to the Church of England separating from the Roman Catholic Church. Before the King James Version, the Geneva Bible contained some notes that were critical of the Church of England and the monarchy, and so seen as problematic to those in power. To mitigate religious conflict, King James sought to standardize Christianity by creating an authoritative English Bible translation. King James did not want anything anti-monarchy in the Bible. For example, he influenced the choice to remove the word *tyrant* from many places in the translation.

The King James Version may also be called the Authorized Version, as it was authorized and commissioned by King James I in 1604. Approximately fifty scholars worked on the translation, crossing out sections of the Bible and writing their suggestions in the margins as they worked. The King James Version was published in 1611.

In time, the language of the King James Version became outdated. But later, people felt the need to return to the good old days by returning to an older way of speaking English, leading to the romanticization of the King James Version. Many bookstores sell largely the KJV because it is in the public domain and is therefore more of a profit-maker for publishers.

King of the Jews

In the century before Jesus's birth, a growing gap between the poor and the wealthy created a group of rebels. This small group grew in anger and in numbers over the decades—a slow burn. The political class felt a need to control this growing group of rebels, and Herod, a Jewish nobleman from Idumea, became the man for the job. In 37 BCE, about four decades before the birth of Jesus, Herod the Great was named King of the Jews. He ruled the Jews with force, controlling any visible signs of a rebellion.

Herod, also a Jew, wanted simultaneously to serve Rome and Judaism. To be accepted by both powers, he rebuilt the Temple. He placed the symbol of Roman power, a golden eagle, over the main body of the Temple, showing his allegiance to the Roman Empire. This is not unlike an American flag hanging in sanctuaries across the United States. Additionally, Herod required the high priest, selected by the Romans, to make daily sacrifices on behalf of Caesar Augustus, who was called the Son of God.

The rebellious anger grew in silence, becoming visible following the death of Herod, the King of the Jews, in 4 BCE. Around the time of his death, a rumor circulated that a child was about to be born who would one day become the King of the Jews.

Indeed, Jesus is estimated to have been born around the time of Herod's death, when the political movement was taking hold of the Jewish people. Romans were using violence to control this political movement. Jesus's teachings were anti-establishment, putting him in harm's way.

The Roman Empire used crucifixion as a punishment mostly for sedition, meaning the inciting of revolt, rebellion, or violence against the established order. The Romans placed plaques above the heads of those dying on crosses to label their crimes, and above Jesus's head read: "King of the Jews." This title was not being used sarcastically or to mock Jesus, but instead was used because the Romans were punishing him for what seemed to be a plan to become king and commit treason.

Jesus was not the only person crucified for sedition and potential treason. There were many people who claimed to be "messiahs" in alignment with the political movement against the Romans and Jewish elite. To claim messianic identity was seen as an intention to declare war on Rome.

Interestingly, in the Gospel of John, Jesus tells Pontius Pilate that those who handed him over to Pilate are more guilty than Pilate himself. John's gospel also states that Pilate, who has a long history of murdering Jews without due process or doubt on his part, gives the crowd a choice: release Jesus or Barabbas. Barabbas was another prisoner to be executed. The name Barabbas in Aramaic means "son of the father."[10] As we are told in the biblical narrative, the crowd chose to free Barabbas over Jesus.

Pilate asks the Jewish people what he should do with their "king," and the Jewish people supposedly reply by saying they have no king but Caesar, a reply that is highly unlikely given the Jewish situation at the time. To give shape to this story that frees Pilate from blame and claims Jews are loyal to Caesar, it is important to remember that the gospels were written decades after the crucifixion of Jesus, and shortly after the Jewish Revolt. John's gospel may have been written in such a way as to keep peace with Roman authorities.

10. Erin K. Vearncombe, Bernard Brandon Scott, and Hal Taussig. *After Jesus Before Christianity: A Historical Exploration of the First Two Centuries of Jesus Movements* (New York: HarperOne, 2021), 93.

Kingdom of God

According to biblical tradition, God promised a homeland to Abraham and Sarah, and later, through the leadership of Miriam and Moses, delivered the Hebrew people from slavery and led them towards a new home for their people. The Book of Joshua presents the story of their arrival and conquest of Canaan. They had specific ideas for how they were going to arrange their shared lives in this land. Then, the Roman Empire conquered them.

Basileia in Greek can be translated as kingdom or empire. The use of language associated with kingdom and empire is important because Jesus lived under the control of an empire. He was intimately aware of the social reality of a powerful empire in a way that is lost on many of us today. "Kingdom of God" is a traditional translation, but another accurate translation is "Empire of God," a clear juxtaposition between the empire the Jews wanted and the Roman Empire they found themselves living under.

The Romans ruled through military force, violence, and heavy taxation. The kingdom of God was an alternative vision to the Roman occupation. The kingdom of God favored the meek and the poor, who were being oppressed by the Romans. The kingdom of God was nonviolent, compassionate, and not self-serving. In many ways, the kingdom of God could be considered the name of the social movement Jesus was a part of.

The gospels of Mark and Luke often use the phrase "Kingdom of God" when referring to the kind of society that God desires for the Israelites. The Gospel of Matthew, however, uses the phrase "kingdom of heavens." In Greek, "heavens" is, in fact, plural. Matthew is referring to the kingdom of God, but he is adhering to Jewish norms by avoiding naming God.

The Pharisees warned Jesus that Herod, the ruler of Galilee, wanted to kill him, and Jesus responded by saying, "Go and tell that fox for me" (Luke 13:31–32). In ancient Jewish culture, to call someone a fox was an insult. Jesus called Herod an imposter, making a clear statement about the kind of kingdom he was bringing. To say the kingdom of God was at hand was another way of saying the end of the Roman Empire is at hand.

In fact, many years after the death of Jesus, the Jews did manage to take back their land from the Romans for four short years. During the first year of their short-lived independence, they had coins made that read "year one,"[11] because they believed it was the first year of God's kingdom on earth. Their liberation from the Romans was brief and ended in extreme violence. Jesus and Paul talked a lot about the kingdom of God. Understanding this statement as a blatant refusal of the Roman way is necessary to understanding who Jesus was.

Kingdom Is Near

Banquets in antiquity differed from our modern parties and gatherings in many ways. Invitations did not contain a date and time to show up; the banquet would occur when the time was right, *kairos*, rather than a time noted on the calendar, *chronos*. Antiquity did not have refrigeration to preserve food, timely delivery systems, or ways to predict

11. Ya'akov Meshorer, *Treasury of Jewish Coins from the Persian Period to Bar Kokhba* (Jerusalem and Nyack, New York: Amphora Books, 2001), chapter 4.

weather conditions. They had to wait until party supplies and food were accessible. The banquet would occur when the time was right. Invitations would say that the banquet was "near." Invited guests would eventually see the banquet being prepared for, and would know the time was finally right.

Similarly, we have many biblical texts stating the kingdom of God is "near." When Jesus tells the parable of the wedding banquet (Matthew 22:1–14 and Luke 14:15–24), the point is not that some people will refuse to attend the king's, or God's, metaphorical banquet. The point is that the wedding banquet, like the kingdom of God, will arrive when conditions are right.

Basilica means "kingdom," but some translate it as "empire" or "dominion." Interestingly, the Romans did not want any talk of a king or kingdom coming near, because they saw kings as failures. It was a clear anti-Rome statement for Jesus to announce a kingdom that is drawing near. Comparing this kingdom to a wedding banquet and stating that the kingdom is near was a way to tell his followers that there is not a specific day or time. Instead, pay attention for the signs of a banquet being prepared. Keep your eyes open for the kingdom of God, because it is closer than you think.

When we see people predicting the time of the apocalypse and the coming kingdom of God, they are revealing a Western bias. The kingdom of God arrives a little at a time—each time compassion is acted out, each time a person's wealth is distributed for the wellbeing of the community. The kingdom of God draws near in these habitual small acts over time. This is how the time, or kairos, becomes right for a banquet and for a kingdom to become reality.

◇◇◇

Legion

Language and symbols can be used to mock, ridicule, and resist power structures. A lot of biblical language is funny, sarcastic, satirical, and seriously irreverent. An example of this hidden meaning can be found in the story of Jesus healing the demoniacs, found in Matthew 8:28–34, Mark 5:1–20, and Luke 8:26–39. It's important to remember that the gospels were written in Greek and largely for a Greek audience, and in Greek psychology emotion was often referred to as a *daimon*. Somebody taken over by strong emotion such as anger or fear was said to be possessed by a *daimon*.

In this story, a sick man appears to be in emotional turmoil and is said to be possessed. He says that his turmoil is caused by a "legion," a word for a large Roman military unit. Additionally, this story is set in northern Israel near where a Roman legion was stationed. The man's possession, or clear emotional suffering, is being caused by this nearby Roman army. When Jesus tells the demon to come out of the man, the demon names itself as "Legion." The story is hiding its true meaning in plain sight, a common way for oppressed groups to make fun of their oppressors. When an oppressed group cannot communicate openly, they create hidden ways to communicate. These secret languages are often called argot or cant in sociology.

The Roman soldiers, or "legion," are demonic, evil, and oppressive in nature. In case the audience for this story missed the creative and hidden use of the label "legion," a pig is also incorporated into the story to drive the point home. The demon is transferred to the pigs in a nearby field. In Hebrew writing, pigs are considered unclean. The meaning, although hidden and not spoken literally, would be clear to those in Jesus's community: Roman soldiers are evil and likened to unclean pigs by Jesus.

If Roman authorities heard this story, proving its meaning would be difficult. A literal understanding of this story would lead us to believe there was a literal exorcism of a literal evil spirit, and Jesus saved the man and the day. Instead, we have Jesus boldly aligning himself against the Roman soldiers and the empire at large. The Romans would label this as treason, a crime punishable by death. In fact, Jesus was later killed for his treasonous teachings and crimes. If you were a person living under Roman occupation and you heard this story, which was in circulation, what you heard was: You are not alone in your suffering at the hands of the Roman Empire, and Jesus is on your side.

Lord

The title "Lord" for God and Jesus has a complex history shaped by translation. The Hebrew word *Adonai* means "my Lord" and is used as a substitute for the divine name *YHWH*. *YHWH* was considered too holy to speak out loud, so when reading scripture in the Jewish tradition, *YHWH* was replaced with *Adonai* to avoid saying the divine name.

In the third to second centuries BCE, the Greek translation of the Hebrew Bible, the Septuagint, translated *Adonai* and *YHWH* as *Kyrios*, meaning "master" or "Lord." The divine title "Lord" became standard in early Christian writings and as a title for Jesus. This had profound theological implications by identifying Jesus with the God of the Hebrew Bible.

Jerome's fourth century CE Latin Vulgate translated *Kyrios* as *Dominus*, meaning "master" or "Lord." To differentiate the earlier use of *YHWH*, many English Bibles will write LORD in all caps.

Referring to God and Jesus as Lord has cultural implications, too. The title Lord was imperial language and was used for Roman emperors. Caesar was said to be Lord. Proclaiming Jesus as Lord was a political statement. It was saying that Jesus was Lord, but it was also saying that Caesar was not. People were told through constant propaganda that the Romans were their Lord and savior. Followers of Jesus were rejecting this political messaging by referring to Jesus as their Lord and savior.

Magdalene

Elizabeth Schrader discusses how she became a New Testament scholar on the podcast *Data over Dogma*. Schrader, a musician, was praying in a garden dedicated to the Virgin Mary and heard an audible response to her prayer: "Maybe you should talk to Mary Magdalene about that." She immediately walked to the library to learn about Mary Magdalene. She later released a record about Mary Magdalene, and continued to learn about her. Long story short, she became a Mary Magdalene expert and scholar.

Part of Schrader's research focused on John 11 and Mary Magdalene, drawing on Papyrus 66. Dated around the year 200 CE, Papyrus 66 is the oldest and most complete text of the Gospel of John. In John 11:1, our English translations of the Bible have the phrase, "the village of Mary and her sister Martha." However, Schrader read the ancient text in its original Greek: "the village of Mary and his sister Mary." The pronouns did not match. What? Schrader zoomed in on the papyrus and saw something that had previously gone unnoticed. The text had been changed.

In Greek, the name Mary is spelled like Maria. Schrader could see that the letter *i* had been changed to the Greek letter *th*, resulting in the second *Mary* of that sentence changing to *Martha*. Additionally, "his" sister was changed to "her" sister. This means that, at some point, a scribe had split Mary into Mary and Martha. Schrader's examination found that every time our English Bibles say "Martha," the original Greek on papyrus said "Mary." Everywhere the original text says "sister," it was changed to "sisters." So, in fact, Martha was added into this text. The editor changed this text to make connections to other biblical texts, but it means we have gotten the story wrong.

Tertullian, who scholar Diana Butler Bass describes as "one of the most misogynistic of all of the ancient church fathers,"[12] wrote a commentary in the early third century on John 11 that says Mary professes Jesus to be the Son of God. However, our English translations give that profession of faith to Martha. Why is this important? There are two confessions of the divine identity of Jesus in the Gospels. One is Peter and, until recently, the other was believed to be Martha. We now know it is Mary. Mary says she believes Jesus is the Messiah who comes into this world. Why would ancient scribes prefer this confession be assigned to Martha rather than Mary? Because Martha is a minor character who "disappears from history,"[13] Bass states. But Mary—assumed to be Mary Magdalene—is a prominent character throughout the Gospels. It is Mary who knows Jesus to be the Messiah. It is Mary Magdalene who is there when Lazarus is raised from the dead; Mary Magdalene identifies Jesus as the Son of God; Mary Magdalene is the person at the grave of Jesus; and Mary Magdalene is the first to see the risen Christ.

The addition of "Magdalene" on Mary's name has been assumed to mean that Mary is from Magdala, not Bethany. However, the connection of Mary to Magdala was not made until the sixth century CE. Furthermore, the village of Magdala was not known during Mary's life. Mag-

12. Wild Goose (Wild Goose Festival), *Sending the Goose with Diana Butler Bass*, YouTube video, 40:54, posted July 22, 2022, https://youtu.be/sSH-nfdh_S0?si=2n-fBcPbjZsNwJsd

13. Wild Goose (Wild Goose Festival), *Sending the Goose with Diana Butler Bass*, YouTube video, 40:54, posted July 22, 2022, https://youtu.be/sSH-nfdh_S0?si=2n-fBcPbjZsNwJsd

dala is not a place of origin, but a title for Mary. In Aramaic, the language Jesus spoke, *Magdalene* means tower. We have Peter the Rock, and we have Mary the Tower. But the John story was changed, and the power of a woman named Mary was hidden from us. It seems likely that somebody preferred to elevate a man's faith—Peter the Rock—over a woman's faith—Mary the Tower.

There is a strong case to be made that Mary Magdalene has a central role in the early church, perhaps playing a bigger role in building up the community than Peter the Rock did. Yet today, we think of Peter as the foundation of the church. We maintain Peter's title of the Rock, while Mary's title of the Tower was hidden for many centuries. In whom do we acknowledge power and in whom would we prefer to hide power?

Mark of the Beast

Amos and Hosea, Hebrew prophets, preach about the Day of the Lord. Isaiah, also a prophet, told the people of Judah that their injustices towards the poor would bring the wrath of God. These prophetic messages spoke of a day when those with power would face justice for their wrongdoings against the poor and marginalized. Those same prophetic messages found their way into the Revelation of John, the concluding book of the Bible.

Some communities of early Jesus followers had a leader named John. Many believe Domitian was responsible for the exile of John to the Greek island of Patmos to weaken the Jesus movement. While in exile during the reign of Domitian, John of Patmos wrote his church communities a letter we now call the Revelation of John. Revelation is full of language, imagery, and symbols his original audiences would have been familiar with.

Revelation has its own cultural context situated in the late first century. John of Patmos was writing to seven specific communities, one being the city of Ephesus. One of the phrases that has taken on life beyond Christianity is the mark of the beast. Ephesus was a city of commerce and ruled by Roman emperors who believed they were gods and demanded to be worshiped. In order to buy and sell, merchants were required to make an incense offering to the Roman emperor, synonymous with claiming the emperor as God. This context is important for varying scholarly perspectives on what the *mark of the beast* meant.

Some argue that after making this offering, worshipers were given a mark of some sort, likely an ink stain on the hand or forehead, to make it known they had pledged their allegiance to and worshiped the emperor and could therefore participate in commerce. A mark on the forehead would have been similar to enslavers branding the enslaved. This mark is known as the mark of the beast. Early Jesus followers believed only Jesus was God incarnate and no other should be worshiped as God. They believed the demand to be worshiped as a God was in alignment with the devil, so taking the mark of the beast was idolatrous.

A less literal interpretation is to view this mark as a sort of seal, or a statement about who you do and do not belong to. This is similar to the cross on the forehead with water or oil during baptism, blood on doorposts to protect as told in Exodus 12, and a man marking the foreheads of those who opposed idolatry and belonged to God in Ezekiel 9:2–4. Either way, refusing to take the mark of the beast was about refusing to participate in the imperial cult of the Roman Empire, which John viewed as idolatry. John, of course, was reminding his communities to stay loyal to Jesus over the empire.

It's necessary that we understand the culturally situated symbolic language used in Revelation. This is not a text predicting the future or a checklist of things that must occur before the second coming of Jesus or the end of the world as we know it. A theology built around a literal understanding of the book has coaxed people into complacency that treats violence around the globe with passive acceptance. For example, countless Christians view violent conflict in the Middle East as necessary; this way of thinking and believing halts humanitarian action. How we read the Bible, including Revelation, has real-life implications.

Scholars have exhaustively explored John's heavy-handed symbolism throughout Revelation. Repeatedly, John is naming the Roman Empire as evil and reminding his communities to stay loyal to Jesus and avoid idolatrous behavior. Idolatry, according to John, is both worshiping other gods and participating in the Roman political and economic system. Revelation is a call to reject a corrupt system that provides riches and power to some while harming and oppressing others.

Revelation's imagery, including the mark of the beast, remains highly debated. John paradoxically writes being against the empire while simultaneously using tools of the empire, like violence and military strength, to discuss God's kingdom. Revelation can be endlessly explored and debated, and there will continue to be mystery in this book. However, John does seem to be making the point that evil is found not primarily in humans, but instead in unjust governments like the Roman Empire and its intersecting systems of worship and commerce that are upheld by complicit humans.

Messiah

Messiah is from the Hebrew word *mashiah*, which means "anointed one." The word *Christ* is Greek and a transliteration for *Messiah*, and Christ became the title given to Jesus. To refer to Jesus as a messiah, or anointed one, had political connotations. Rulers were anointed when they began their reign. This connection between Messiah, Christ, and anointed one is often lost today because of its linguistic history.

The Messiah is connected to the Davidic prophecy, which is a belief that a descendant of King David would eventually come to rule and bring peace once again. Under King David's rule, there was relative peace and prosperity. This prophecy was, in many ways, a political prophecy as much as a religious prophecy. King David unified the twelve tribes of Israel into a single kingdom, making him one of the most beloved figures of Jewish history. King David cannot be glorified without putting him in his rightful context. He had faults and sins, too. For example, he abused his power, impregnated Bathsheba, and arranged the death of her husband. Nevertheless, he is remembered in history for his political and military accomplishments that brought unification and a time of peace. King Solomon did not keep this legacy in place, so people craved another ruler like King David. This expected "anointed one" became the expected Messiah who would bring peace once again.

Many kings and queens continue to be anointed when they take the throne. Similarly, many priests, pastors, and other clergy are anointed with oil when they are ordained into their leadership role. This connection between the Messiah identity and anointing remains intact not only when we look at the linguistic connections, but also in the practice of baptism. Baptism incorporates many earthly elements, including water, fire, and oil. Many Christian traditions immerse the person being baptized in water. A baptismal candle is often lit and given to the person. Additionally, the baptized person is anointed with oil in the sign of the cross on the forehead. This is a tactile practice pointing back to the Messiah as the Anointed One. Baptized Christians are being anointed into the community of faith, just as Jesus is considered the Anointed One, or Messiah.

Myrrh

There are many mentions of contraceptives throughout the Bible, if we understand the euphemistic shape of the language. For example, the Book of Esther tells a story of Esther saving the Jewish people from genocide by hiding her Jewish identity and seducing the Persian king to become queen. Esther 2:12 describes many women, including Esther, to be anointed with myrrh for an entire year before seeing the king. Of course, "seeing the king" was a euphemism for having sex with the king. These women do not want to become pregnant, nor does the king want to impregnate each woman who comes to "see" him.

Myrrh was a known contraceptive. We know this because a Greek physician and expert in gynecology named Soranus of Ephesus wrote about myrrh as birth control sometime during the first two centuries CE.[14] I find it especially interesting that the Book of Esther tells the story of a woman taking control over the harm that is intended on her people while also taking control over her own body by applying a contraceptive to avoid pregnancy.

Women's voices, perspectives, and knowledge were often suppressed during the creation of the Bible. Women had their own codes and medical practices passed from generation to generation, from grandmother to mother to daughter. Women found ways to protect themselves from the unwanted pregnancies and they shared this knowledge with each other.

We find traces of this preserved knowledge in Esther, and in other places throughout the Bible. In Song of Solomon, some of the plants discussed, such as pomegranates, myrrh, and cinnamon, were used by

14. Laurence Totelin, "Old Recipes, New Practice? The Latin Adaptations of the Hippocratic Gynaecological Treatises," *Social History of Medicine* 24, no. 1 (2011): 74–91, https://doi.org/10.1093/shm/hkq103.

women as contraceptives. The man offers these contraceptives to the woman, just as any person wishing to avoid pregnancy would do.

Numbers 5:11–22 states that if the woman has been unfaithful, this "water of bitterness" will bring the "curse" into her "bowels," make the woman's uterus drop and womb discharge, and bring her "bitter pain." If this pain does not come, it will prove that there was, in fact, no fetus to abort and the wife was not unfaithful after all. The English Standard Version of Numbers 5 says, "May this water that brings the curse pass into your bowels and make your womb swell and your thigh fall away." Within Judaism, the thigh is a euphemism for the uterus. Some interpret this to be an incident of abortion. Abortion is one way to interpret Numbers 5. However, there are other ways to understand this text. For example, some read this as not an intentional miscarriage but as an intentional damaging to the uterus so the woman can no longer conceive if she has been unfaithful. The punishment, in this interpretation, is not the miscarriage or abortion of the fetus, but the inability to become pregnant in the future. The Hebrew makes this text somewhat ambiguous and perhaps inappropriate to the abortion debate.

The conversation surrounding women's issues, especially concerning sexuality, in the Bible has not been central in the Christian discourse. "Women found themselves in one of two roles: (aspiring) wife/mother or mistress/prostitute."[15] However, the Protestant Reformation put the Bible into the hands, homes, and languages of many women, resulting in women's interpretations complicating historically dominant interpretations.

◇◇◇

15. Amanda W. Benckhuysen, *The Gospel According to Eve: A History of Women's Interpretation* (Downers Grove, IL: InterVarsity Press, 2019), 99.

Nazareth

Jesus of Nazareth was born into a family of Jews in Roman-occupied Palestine two thousand years ago, a dangerous time and place in imperial history. Understanding Jesus's hometown of Nazareth is vital for understanding Jesus's life and worldview.

Nazareth was a small, rural village located in lower Galilee. Scholars widely disagree on the population of Nazareth, but the mid-range estimate is a few hundred people or less than one hundred Jewish families. The village of Nazareth lacked roads, contained one shared bath of collected rainwater for the entire population, and consisted of illiterate peasants who made a living mostly as farmers and day laborers. Nazarenes, like Jesus and his family, lived in two-room homes, and probably could not afford consistent carpentry or labor Jesus was offering.

This means Jesus likely left Nazareth to find work as a carpenter by traveling to Galilee's capital city of Sepphoris, a city within walking distance of Nazareth. Sepphoris was a wealthy Jewish city with two-story homes, large public baths with plenty of water, a Roman theater that could seat over 4,000 people, and paved roads everywhere.

Understanding that Jesus was from Nazareth and likely traveled regularly to Sepphoris for work is vital to understanding his ministry. Jesus grew up seeing his family and neighbors being oppressed by the system of Roman rule. He witnessed the discrepancies between scarce resources in Nazareth compared to the more plentiful resources in places like Sepphoris. His teachings were fueled by his childhood and experiences in Nazareth.

New Revised Standard Version

The New Revised Standard Version (NRSV) is a widely respected English translation of the Bible. The NRSV is a revision of the Revised Standard Version (RSV), which was itself a revision of the American Standard Version (ASV) (1901), a descendant of the King James Version (KJV). The NRSV was first published in 1989.

The NRSV is known for its more inclusive language, especially in reference to gender. For example, where original texts use masculine terms only, like "brothers," the NRSV uses "brothers and sisters." Additionally, translators of the NRSV, which included scholars from multiple denominations and Judaism, were intentional about their efforts to incorporate the latest biblical scholarship and insights from manuscript discoveries like that of the Dead Sea Scrolls.

The NRSV is used widely among Protestants, Catholics, and even Eastern Orthodox Christians. Translation is work that has no end, because language is always evolving. A new revision, called the NRSV Updated Edition (NRSVue), was released in 2021. As of the summer of 2025, mainline Protestant Revised Common Lectionaries use the NRSVue translation, meaning scripture readings during worship services in these churches now come from the NRSVue.

Offerings (See Sacrifice)

Palm Branches

The seventh chapter of the Gospel of John is about the Festival of Tabernacles, one of the major Hebrew feasts. On the eighth and final day of this festival, the high priest would pour water and wine together and the thousands of gathered people would chant: *Hosanna! Hosanna! Hosanna* means "God save us now!" When Jesus rode on a donkey into Jerusalem, people cheered: *Hosanna! Hosanna!* While cheering, palm branches were waved and laid on the ground as Jesus entered Jerusalem.

Palm branches also figure in the story of Judas Maccabaeus, a Jewish leader in the second century BCE, whose arrival in Jerusalem was also marked by the waving of palm branches. Judas revolted against the empire, which ultimately led to the rededication of the Second Temple in Jerusalem. Judas defeated the Syrian king and ruled. Although the Romans recaptured the city a century later, the palm branches symbolized the people's expectations of Jesus. They were expecting another military revolt and for him to become an empire ruler.

The palm branches are foundational to Palm Sunday, the Sunday before Easter when we commemorate Jesus entering Jerusalem. People waved palm branches upon Jesus's arrival. Years after the death of Jesus, palm branches were used for Emperor Hadrian. When he traveled through his empire, people would make sacrifices to him and pray at his feet. Coins with palm branches were made in Hadrian's honor to symbolize the belief in him as a savior.

The palm branches came to signify a savior. When we go to church on Palm Sunday and take Communion, shout "*Hosanna! Hosanna!*," and wave palm branches, we are engaging in a profound protest against the empire. We are saying that the way of Jesus is the true path of power. We are rejecting violence and conquering and war and oppression. We are turning towards peace and love of neighbor and love of enemy.

Pharisees

During Jesus s life, there were several Jewish sects, among them the Pharisees, the Sadducees, the Herodians, the Essenes, and the Zealots. The Pharisees, which means "Separate Ones," was possibly a title given to the group by their enemies. The Pharisees had strict interpretations of the Torah and religious tradition. They were known as the expert interpreters of the Law, or Torah. They believed in an afterlife, resurrection, and angels. While they interpreted the Torah, they also focused on purity laws and oral tradition.

Jesus frequently criticized the Pharisees. For example, Jesus spoke against their rigid focus on religious observance while neglecting justice and mercy (Matthew 23:23–38), and their strict view of the Sabbath (Mark 2:23–28; Luke 13:10–17). However, there were also commonalities between Jesus and the Pharisees. For example, both took the Hebrew Scriptures seriously (Matthew 5–7).

We often think of Judaism during Jesus's time as having a unified vision and interpretation of the faith, but this is untrue. Like today's Christianity, there were many variants of Judaism, each with their own sets of beliefs, practices, and political alignment.

Privy

Jesus said it is not what enters a person that makes them unclean, but instead what comes out of them (Matthew 15:11). His disciples needed clarity about this teaching, so Jesus explained again that what enters a person does not go into their heart, but instead enters their bowels and then passes out into the privy. Sometimes this word is also translated as sewer, but both are inaccurate translations that miss the tone that accompanies this term. In Matthew, the word *aphedron* is used, which is Macedonian slang and more closely translated as "shithole."[16] The word Jesus used is like "shithole" to our modern ears, much more impolite and vulgar.

Trinitarian theology states that Jesus was not fifty percent human and fifty percent divine, but instead fully human and fully divine. Understanding that Jesus sometimes used profane or harsh language is important. It reinforces Jesus's full humanity and challenges sometimes-sanitized Christian norms. Christianity often elevates polite language as virtuous, but Jesus was sometimes offensive. Righteous anger, as demonstrated by Jesus's language, is both human and divine.

A preference for clean language is not problematic. However, sometimes respectability, especially through our language, is elevated as an idol. For Christians, Jesus is God incarnate, and Jesus the Christ used disrespectful and impolite language from time to time to help him make his rhetorical points. This does not make him less human, but fully human.

Prophet

The word prophet comes from the Latin word *prophetizare* and Greek word *prophēteuō*. It is a compound word containing *pro*, meaning "before," and *phētēs*, meaning "one who declares." Literally, a prophet is somebody who declares before. Over time, the word prophet has picked

16. Thomas Cahill, *Desire of the Everlasting Hills: The World Before and After Jesus* (New York: Nan A. Talese / Anchor Books, 1999), 88-89.

up a strong association with the telling of the future. However, there is a lot more to a prophet than telling the future. A prophet has everything to do with the connections between the past, present, and future.

The shift in how we view a prophet has been influenced by ancient Hebrew culture, ancient Greek culture, and our English-speaking culture. In the Hebrew Bible, or Old Testament, the word *navi'* is often translated as prophet, and it primarily referred to a deliverer of divine messages. These messages often contained moral warnings about what would happen if a given path was not changed. In ancient Greek culture, a prophet was, first and foremost, one who spoke on behalf of the gods. Often this involved predictions about the future, but it also included messages for the present moment. Eventually, "prophet" entered the English-speaking world through Middle English, and it was primarily associated with predicting the future.

People at the top or near the top of the socioeconomic hierarchy are often blind to the struggles of those at the bottom. In the nineteenth and early twentieth centuries, coal miners were in constant risk of exposure to toxic gases. Canaries were highly sensitive to these gases and would show signs of struggle, or even die, before the levels became high enough to harm humans. Coal miners would pay attention to the canaries brought into the mines for signs of danger. People at the bottom of the hierarchy are the canaries in the coal mine. Marginalized communities experience the harm of a broken society first, and the ability to listen to the sensitivities and wisdom of the marginalized is, in itself, a form of wisdom. Prophets, who are often on the bottom of the hierarchy or can align with the perspectives of those at the bottom, are canaries in the coal mine.

Prophets come in many forms, but they are always addressing the issue of power and oppression. In his foundational book, *The Prophetic Imagination*, Walter Brueggeman writes, "The task of prophetic ministry is to nurture, nourish, and evoke a consciousness and perception alternative to the consciousness and perception of the dominant culture around us."[17] This is true of prophetic voices today, and it is true of prophetic voices in the Bible. There are many prophets in the Bible, including Amos, Isaiah, Jeremiah, and Elijah. Amos spoke against systemic injustice when he denounced the exploitation of the poor by condemning those who "sell the innocent for silver, and the needy for a pair of sandals" (Amos 2:6). Isaiah condemned rulers who "make iniquitous decrees," "write oppressive statutes," "turn aside the needy," and "rob the poor" (Isaiah 10:1–2). Jeremiah accused leaders of failing to defend those who are oppressed by stating, "Do justice and righteousness, and deliver from the hand of the oppressor him who has been robbed" (Jeremiah 22:3). Elijah confronted King Ahab and Queen Jezebel for exploiting those without power (1 Kings 21).

For many Christians, the Davidic and messianic prophecies are the most familiar. This, too, came out of oppression and the need for hope. These prophecies were just as political as they were religious. King David unified the twelve tribes of Israel into a single kingdom, making him one of the most beloved figures of Jewish history. King David cannot be glorified without putting him in his rightful context. He had faults and sins, too.

After David's reign, Israel began to decline. David's son, Solomon, ruled after him, and toward the end of Solomon's life, the kingdom was divided again. Solomon significantly strayed from Moses's prophetic reality.

The northern kingdom of Israel was conquered by the Assyrians because of political and religious corruption. The southern kingdom of Judah fell to the Babylonians. People longed for a future king like David, back when there was unity rather than division. This is how the prophecy

17. Walter Brueggemann, *The Prophetic Imagination: 40th Anniversary Edition* (Minneapolis: Fortress Press: 2018), chap. 1, Kindle.

took hold. A new messiah, or anointed king, would come to bring peace and unity once again, and this messiah would come from the line of David.

We see a pattern in prophetic messages. Many prophetic messages are about God's desire to liberate people from oppression. The entire Bible is about liberation from oppression. Not only are prophets aligning with the oppressed, but they are often speaking truth to power by speaking against kings, priests, and the wealthy. Prophets challenge systems that benefit a few while harming the many. Prophets do not tell the future. They tell the truth. People don't like the truth, especially when they are benefiting from the current arrangements. This is why many prophets have been murdered. Those with power will go to far lengths to silence prophetic voices. Jeremiah was imprisoned and nearly killed (Jeremiah 38:6). Zechariah was murdered in the Temple (2 Chronicles 24:20–21). Jesus was killed on the cross.

It is easy to see how our understanding of prophets evolved to be seen as those who can predict future events. Oftentimes, they are warning those in power that the system is broken, and these warnings are accompanied by a wise telling of the destruction to come if the system is not remedied or even dismantled altogether. Prophets are voices of hope. Daniel's visions encouraged Jews who were living under oppressive empires. Ezekiel gave hope by reassuring the exiled Israelites that their oppression was temporary. Of course, prophets are not only something of the past. Father Richard Rohr discusses the importance of ongoing prophetic ministries in his book *The Tears of Things: Prophetic Wisdom for an Age of Outrage*. Prophets, first and foremost, see current wrongs and speak of hope for a better possible future.

Purity Rituals

Ritual purity laws are religious regulations about a person's state of purity, a determination of whether or not a person was allowed to participate in sacred activities, like worship. Paul, among others, argued that these purity laws were no longer needed, so many Christians today do not see the cultural importance of these rituals.

There are many ritual purity laws in the Hebrew Bible, primarily in Leviticus and Numbers. These laws state when a person is considered impure and unclean, and how they can become pure and clean again. These rituals often involve washing oneself, waiting a period of time, and making sacrifices. At first glance, these laws may appear outdated and pointless.

It is vital to understand these laws were related primarily to death and sexuality. Ritual purity practices surrounding death were related to proximity to a dead body. Numbers 19:11–22 says that one who touches a dead body is unclean for seven days, as long as they are purified with water mixed with the ashes of a red heifer on the third and seventh days. Leviticus 21:1–4 forbids priests from touching a dead body, unless it was a close family member. Leviticus 22:4–6 states a priest who touches a dead body must wash and becomes unclean until evening. Exposure to death was seen as being in a state of impurity for a time.

Ritual purity practices surrounding sexuality were related to sexual activity, menstruation, and childbirth. The Israelites had to be cleansed when they engaged in sexual activity; experienced or were exposed to the blood of menstruation; or experienced or were exposed to the process of childbirth. Leviticus 15:19–30 states that a woman on her period is ritually unclean for seven days. Additionally, anything she touches—her bed, chairs, and clothes—is also unclean. Anyone who touches her or these objects are considered unclean until evening. Leviticus 12:1–8 says when a woman gives birth, she is unclean for seven days if she births a son and for fourteen days if she births a daughter. Before entering the sanctuary, she must undergo a longer purification period and bring an offering. It isn't just women who are deemed unclean at times. Leviticus 15:16–18 says that when a man "has an emission of semen," he is unclean until evening and must bathe in water. Similarly, when a man has abnormal discharge, he is unclean for seven days and is required to undergo a seven-day purification period and offer a sacrifice. When people engage in sexual activity, they must wash and are ritually unclean until evening. Like death, exposure to sexuality was seen as being in a state of impurity for a time.

These laws shaped how individuals and communities moved through cycles of impurity and restoration, which created sacred rhythms that structured life. It is not a coincidence that many of the purification periods lasted seven days, given that the number seven has a symbolic connection to completion and perfection.

More important, these ritual purity laws surrounding exposure to death and sexuality were intentional and strategic. When the Israelites wandered in the desert, they were caught between two identities—the Egyptians who had enslaved them for many generations and the Canaanites of their future. The Egyptians worshiped over the dead and the Canaanites worshiped through sexuality. It is no mistake the Israelites in the desert were instructed to participate in rituals of cleanliness when they were exposed to death and sexuality. Death and sexuality were not seen as problematic. On the contrary, death and sexuality were intimate and unavoidable parts of life. Instead, engaging in rituals that cleansed them of their exposure to death and sexuality ensured they did not worship over death or through sexuality, like the nations of their past and future.

Through these purity practices, the Israelites were called to form a unified identity in the present moment. This identity separated them from the ways of their enslavers in Egypt and the ways of the Canaanites they would experience in their future. They had to be cleansed from the possibility they would adopt the Egyptian or Canaanite ways of worshiping. They needed a new way.

Sacrifice

All sacrifices are offerings, but not all offerings are sacrifices. Offerings are anything given to God, while a sacrifice is an offering that has a loss or cost involved. Sacrifice comes from the words *sacrum*—meaning "sacred"—and *facere*—meaning "to make." Literally, to sacrifice is to make something sacred, often by offering it to God. To make food sacred in ancient times was vital, as food was not always readily available. Sacrificing an animal before eating it made it sacred and ready for consumption. Throughout our history, humans have communed by preparing and consuming food together. To sacrifice animals in this way is to commune with God.

Leviticus provides specific instructions for how to conduct animal sacrifices. If the idea of animal sacrifice seems outdated and problematic to you, it is important to remember that our capitalist culture abuses animals in many ways, including: keeping chickens in overcrowded and unnatural environments; physically mutilating pigs and cows by docking their tails; castrating various animals without anesthesia; breeding animals to grow unnaturally fast, resulting in many health issues; denying animals food and water on long transports to slaughterhouses; and slaughtering animals in painful and inhumane ways. Animal sacrifice did not involve these sorts of abusive practices. In ancient times, sacrifices of animals were made at the altar in order to invite God into the meal. Sometimes the person making the offering would eat the meal, and sometimes the meal was for the priests. These sacrificed animals were killed and eaten. We continue to kill and eat animals today, but today we neglect and abuse them first—all in the name of production, overconsumption, and profit.

The specificities of the animals being sacrificed in Leviticus are telling. The Israelites are instructed to make sacrifices of animals—like ram, bull, and cow. These are animals that symbolized Egyptian gods. The ram was associated with Amun, a powerful god in Egypt often depicted with ram's horns. The bull was considered sacred in Egypt and was associated with Apis, who was depicted as a black bull with white markings. The Egyptian goddess Hathor was depicted as a woman with cow horns. Instead of worshiping these animals the way their enslavers did, the Israelites were instructed to slaughter the animal and offer it to their God.

These practices of animal sacrifice ensured that they were not reenacting the ways of their Egyptian enslavers by worshiping these specific animals. The Israelites sacrificed these animals to make a symbolic break from the ways of their Egyptian enslavers. The Israelites sacrificed these animals to break free from their past and ensure they were worshiping the God who liberated them from enslavement rather than worshipping the familiar gods of their enslavers.

Offerings also manifest an economic hierarchy. Leviticus 4:3 tells us that if an anointed priest sins, he must offer a bull. Leviticus 4:22–28 states that when a ruler sins, he must offer a male goat, and when any common people sin, they must offer a female goat. Leviticus 4:32 says that a sheep offering is also acceptable. Things get interesting in Leviticus 5:7, when the text says, "But if you cannot afford a sheep, you shall bring to the LORD . . . two turtle-doves or two pigeons." Leviticus 5:11 goes on to say, "But if you cannot afford two turtle-doves or two pigeons, you shall bring . . . one-tenth of an ephah of choice flour . . . you shall not put oil on it or lay frankincense on it."

Interestingly, these people had recently been rescued from Egypt. They did not have riches, wealth, or even an established economic system. And yet, they were already beginning to rank themselves. But at the same time, God proclaims that the ranking allows everyone to have access. If you can't afford a bull, goat, or sheep, then bring some birds. If birds prove inaccessible to anybody, then even choice flour is accepted—not even the finest flour with oil or frankincense, but any flour will do.

This is a God accessible to everybody, not just the priests and rulers with cows, goats, and sheep. In the ancient Near East, this kind of God was unheard of. Everybody has access to flour, and this is a God even the oppressed can be in relationship with. The use of flour as an offering by the Israelites in the wilderness helps us define what kind of God we are dealing with: a God aware of the oppressed and accessible to those on the bottom of the human-made hierarchy.

Sacrifice is related to atonement because sacrifices were often made to restore a broken relationship between God and/or neighbors. Atonement, or *kippur*, means "to cover" or "to purge." The Day of Atonement, or Yom Kippur, is connected to sacrifice and national atonement. Living sacrifices were common because blood was considered to be a life force.

Sacrifice and atonement are related to some theological views of Jesus's death on the cross. Substitutionary atonement theory views his death as a sort of sacrifice or atonement for sins. Some Christians see Jesus's death as a way to make humanity's relationship with God right again.

Ancient Israel's sacrificial systems evolved over time. Language related to offerings and sacrifices have made their way into more recent historical tragedies. The word "holocaust" has its roots in the language for burnt offering, the Hebrew *'olah* and Greek *holokautoma*, meaning "a complete burning."

Historically, people offered animals, oil, grains, and wine to worship and commune with God, or gods. These sacrifices were often viewed as an atonement for sins and sometimes involved a communal feast as a peace offering to communities who might have been harmed by another's sin. After the Temple period, tithing became a primary system of offering. *Tithe* comes from the word meaning "tenth," and tithing was the gift of a tenth of the harvest to support the priests and the poor. Sacrifices are a type of ritualistic offering associated with sins, while tithing became a system of offering that helped support the overall community.

The history and meaning behind sacrifices is as complex as the history and meaning of religion itself. It deserves to be viewed within this complexity. It is a mistake to view history only through a modern moralistic lens. The violence must be simultaneously denounced and put in its rightful cultural contexts.

Sadducees

DURING JESUS'S LIFE, there were several Jewish sects, among them the Pharisees, the Sadducees, the Herodians, the Essenes, and the Zealots. Of these groups, we know the least about the Sadducees. The Sadducees, the priestly elite, were more aligned with ruling powers and associated with Temple worship. Unlike the Pharisees, they believed in no afterlife, and they rejected the oral tradition. They only accepted the Torah, and they were known to collaborate with the Roman authorities to maintain order. The Sadducees lost power after the destruction of the Temple in 70 CE.

These are only a few of the Jewish sects of that day. We often think of Judaism during Jesus's time as having a unified vision and interpretation of the faith, but this is untrue. Like today's Christianity, there were many variants of Judaism, each with their own sets of beliefs, practices, and political alignment.

Salt of the Earth

In the Sermon on the Mount Jesus says: "You are the salt of the earth" (Matthew 5:13). The "you" here is plural, and he is referring to his disciples.

The word "salt" comes from the Latin *sel.* Roman soldiers were-sometimes paid monthly in a payment called a *salarium*, from the root *sel.* To underscore this point, Roman soldiers were paid in—you guessed it—salt. This is where we get our English word *salary*. We can see that salt and salary are related.

With salt as a soldier's payment, to call the disciples the salt of the earth is a comment about a new kind of military, although not a literal military. Jesus was drawing a parallel between his community and the Roman soldiers.

The Cambridge Dictionary defines this phrase as an idiom for "very good, honest, and reasonable, and not thinking you are special in any way." In a culture where salt is plentiful and common, it is understandable that salt of the earth can be taken to mean "not special." However, Jesus is not talking to us; he is talking to his first century disciples who were living when salt was not plentiful and common. To be the salt of the earth means to be of value. Understanding the socioeconomic realities of Jesus's time are necessary for interpretation here, as in most parts of the Bible.

◇◇◇

Samaritan

As Jesus was teaching one day, a lawyer asked him the question: Who is my neighbor? Jesus answered with what we know as the Parable of the Good Samaritan (Luke 10:25–37). The parable goes like this:

A man was stripped naked and beaten by robbers in Jericho, and a priest passed by him on the other side of the street. Similarly, the Levite, a priestly assistant in the Temple, saw him and passed by on the other side of the street. However, when a Samaritan saw him, the Samaritan stopped to take care of him. He went so far as to take the injured man to an inn and pay for his medical care. Jesus makes his point clear by saying the Samaritan is more a neighbor to the beaten man than the priest or Levite.

The Samaritans were hated by the Jews. Samaritans were viewed as impure and socially problematic. Although the Jews and Samaritans worshiped the same God, the Samaritans were largely hated by the Jews because instead of worshiping the God of Israel in the Temple, they worshiped on Mount Gerizim. These groups had many differences, but they also had many religious similarities, including their monotheistic beliefs, shared ancestry, and adherence to the Torah. As is often the case, similarities can create deeper enemies than differences can. For example, Christians have more conflict with Jews, Muslims, and other Christians than they do with Hindus or Buddhists.

Understanding this division between the Jewish people and the Samaritans shifts the way we interpret the Parable of the Good Samaritan. Jesus was decentralizing the Temple as the only holy authority and showing kindness and inclusion even to the disliked Samaritans. The

Samaritans, who worshipped outside the Temple, act in a more loving and God-like way than the priests of the Temple in Jerusalem. Jesus is teaching a kindness that extends to anybody we meet on our path.

Savior

The pharaohs and rulers of ancient Egypt were often called the saviors of their people and considered gods. With each new ruler came promises of salvation sent directly from the heavens: healing the sick, feeding the hungry, clothing the naked.

There is a long history of those with power parading as saviors. *Savior* was also a common title given to Roman emperors, a linguistic reminder that they were tasked with saving people from chaos. The Priene Calendar inscription contains titles for Augustus, including "Savior of all." Augustus announced that he was God incarnate sent to spread peace and prosperity. He even had a twelve-day celebration, called *Advent*, to acclaim his arrival as God incarnate. During this celebration, songs and hymns were sung and coins were created that read: "There is no name save Augustus by which men can be saved."[18] Despite constant propaganda, citizens realized the emperor was not able to provide the salvation they needed to survive and thrive. They needed another source of salvation.

The title of *Savior* was given to Jesus by his early followers. In fact, the Hebrew word *Yeshua* means "to rescue" or "salvation." The idea that salvation came from Jesus was deeply countercultural, considering

18. Rob Bell, "Jesus, Domitian and The Book of Revelation," filmed 2018, YouTube video, posted by John JP Patterson, 10:20, May 16, 2018, https://youtu.be/uThyuSy8CsM?si=CiuyJR1dyUmGkdrv

salvation was commonly believed to come from a king or emperor who ruled through violent conquering and a strong militia. Gods were considered to be warriors and conquerors. Jesus, however, was tortured and crucified. To believe that salvation comes through Jesus rather than the emperor was a bold statement against the Roman Empire.

Serpent

While the earliest Epic of Gilgamesh stories predate the earliest biblical stories by about nine hundred years, there are many similarities between the two. For example, in the Epic of Gilgamesh, the goddess Ishtar had a tree of life that was guarded by a serpent, and Genesis also includes a tree and snake. Gilgamesh sees his friend die and decompose, so he seeks eternal life; a snake ultimately snatches it away from him. Similarly, the snake plays a role in Adam and Eve losing eternal life.

We often think of snakes when we think about serpents, but creatures like dragons and sea monsters are also considered serpents in many cultures and mythologies. Although the symbol of a serpent is well known in Genesis, serpents are discussed throughout the Bible. Moses's staff becomes a serpent (Exodus 4:3), the wilderness the Israelites are journeying through is said to contain serpents (Deuteronomy 8:15), and enemy nations are discussed using serpent imagery (Isaiah 14:29, 30:6). The New Testament discusses serpents, too: John the Baptist and Jesus refer to some religious leaders as a brood of vipers (Matthew 3:7, 23:33), Jesus tells his disciples they will tread on serpents (Luke 10:19), and Satan is compared to a serpent (Revelation 12:9, 20:2).

The image of the serpent has a long history. In pre-biblical cultures, the serpent often represented fertility or wisdom. For example, the god

Ningishzida was depicted with serpents and was strongly associated with cycles of death, rebirth, and nature's fertility. The shedding skin of snakes makes them a clear symbol for death and renewal. In the Hebrew Bible and the New Testament, the serpent often signifies deception and danger. However, the serpent has nuanced symbolic meanings and is also used to convey judgment and healing. Although healing and judgment may seem to contradict one another, divine judgment is theologically wrapped up in divine healing and transformation.

The most popularized serpent is in Genesis. Many interpret the serpent in Genesis, *nachash* in Hebrew, to be the devil. However, there is nothing in Genesis that clearly states this. Instead, later New Testament writers seemingly interpreted the snake to be the devil, especially in Revelation 20:2, which likens the ancient serpent to the devil and Satan. The idea that the devil plays a part in Adam's sin wasn't clearly expressed until the second century by Justin Martyr.

Adding a snake to the creation narrative gives a clue to modern readers (and ancient listeners) that this story contains metaphorical meaning. There are many possible reasons the story includes a snake to entice Eve. As in the Epic of Gilgamesh, the snake could be a symbol of immortality. The poisonous nature of many snakes could have also made it the ideal symbol for deception and danger. The choice to use a snake could have also been linguistic and poetic, since various Semitic languages use the word *chivya* for snake and the similar word *chavah* for Eve. No matter the reason, serpents were used in nuanced ways in the biblical texts.

Seven and Seventy

We read in Genesis the world was created in six days, and then God rested on the seventh day. This established a cycle we continue to live within today. Building on that model, every seventh year was a Sabbatical year of rest for the land. After seven cycles of seven years, or forty-nine years, the fiftieth year is the Jubilee, which is a time when debts were to be forgiven, enslaved people were to be freed, and ancestral lands were to be returned to their original families. The Sabbath, Sabbatical year, and Jubilee are practices in which the numbers seven and seventy are used as a symbol of divine cycles of time related to rest and liberation.

The Israelites were instructed to set up their political and social systems in a way that ensured regular rest, forgiveness, restoration, and liberation. And yet, these systems that ensured equity and freedom were eventually forgotten. The Israelites became enslaved once again, this time to the Babylonians. In Jeremiah 25:11–12, the writer says God will serve the king of Babylon for seventy years. The writer's use of the number seventy demonstrates that the Israelites' enslavement to the Babylonians will inevitably be a part of a cycle of events that will end in liberation, similar to that of the Sabbath, Sabbatical year, and Jubilee.

We see the reminder of liberation in the symbolic numbers of seven and seventy embedded into the Israelites' history. Genesis 10 lists seventy nations, pointing to the completeness of humanity. Numbers 11 states Moses appointed seventy elders. Leviticus 23 tells us they had seven feasts. Leviticus 16:14 tells us the priests sprinkled blood seven times for atonement. Jericho's walls fell after seven days of marching. Revelation, a book full of symbolic meaning, is filled with the number seven—seven churches, seven seals, seven trumpets, etc. In Luke 10:1, Jesus sends out seventy disciples.

Daniel speaks about seventy weeks, or sets of seven years, referring to God's timeline for restoration. Again, we see the connection between the numbers seven and seventy, and the themes of restoration, renewal, and liberation. Similar to Jeremiah and elsewhere in the Bible, when we see the numbers seven or seventy in relation to time, it is not always a literal telling of time. Instead, it is a hint to biblical audiences that liberation is coming. In other words, when we see the numbers seven or seventy, we know there is hope.

In Matthew 18:21–22, Jesus tells Peter to forgive seventy times seven. These are not random numbers. Jesus was a student of the Torah. He was intimately familiar with God's instructions to observe the Sabbath, Sabbatical year, and Jubilee. Jesus references the numbers seven and seventy to point to these teachings, some of which his fellow Jews were forgetting once again. Jesus was reminding Peter that God gave Israel liberation and forgiveness—and these two things go hand-in-hand—every seven days, seven years, and seven cycles of seven years. Jesus was telling Peter that he must forgive as God has forgiven. Forgiveness is not just an internal state; it is built into the very structures of our world. This is how we bring the kingdom of God here on earth.

The Hebrew word for seven is *sheva*, which is related to the word *shava*, meaning "oath." God makes an oath to restore all things that suffer. The Hebrew verb for making a covenant or oath meant literally "to seven oneself," which was followed by repeating an act or ritual seven times. We see this in Genesis 21:25–34, which states that Abraham and Abimelech made a covenant and Abraham set apart seven ewe lambs as part of this practice. When we see the number seven in the Bible, it is not always a literal measurement of time. Instead, it is a story of God promising to bring liberation.

Slaves of God

The New Testament is full of enslavement language. Followers of Jesus were often referred to as "slaves," or *douloi*, of God. The phrase "slaves of God" reads differently when we understand that the original audience for these texts included enslaved people, formerly enslaved people, and those who could soon need to sell themselves into enslavement for their own economic survival. Furthermore, it reads differently when we know that enslaved people in the Roman Empire, who ranked lowest on the hierarchy of Roman socioeconomic status, often collaborated in the making and spreading of the Jesus stories as scribes, copyists, and lectors.

Acts 16 tells the story of an enslaved woman following Paul and crying out, "These men are slaves of the Most High God" (Acts 16:17). To be a slave of God was subversive language against the enslavers. This is especially compelling when we consider that both enslaved and enslavers were members of early Jesus communities. To be a slave of God was to be obedient to a way of life beyond the orders of your Roman enslaver. It meant belonging to God, not your Roman enslaver.

The New Testament's language of enslavement may have been used to empower the enslaved within early Jesus communities. Nevertheless, this language has been used by later Christians in positions of power to justify enslavement. The Bible has been used by those with power to inflict evil on many humans throughout history, and this part of Christianity's history cannot be overlooked for comfort's sake.

In 1 Kings 9:15, we are told that King Solomon used slave labor to build the Temple. The Temple is being built to honor the God who liberated the Israelites from slave labor, but they are using slave labor to build this Temple. We often forget our history and end up oppressing others in the same way we were oppressed.

To justify the enslavement of Africans, our ancestors pointed to biblical texts. Leviticus 25:44–46 says, "As for the male and female slaves whom you may have, it is from the nations around you that you may acquire male and female slaves. You may also acquire them from among the aliens residing with you . . . and they may be your property." In Paul's epistle to the Ephesians (6:5), he says, "Slaves, obey your earthly masters with fear and trembling." Similarly, Colossians 3:22 instructs slaves to obey their earthly masters. Additionally, 1 Timothy 6:1–2 and Titus 2:9–10 seem to support slavery. There is no shortage of biblical texts used to justify slavery in the United States of America. Interestingly, slave owners and abolitionists used not only the same Bible to support their arguments, but often the same verses—further evidence that rather than finding our values from sacred texts, we bring our values to our readings of sacred texts.

Just as the Israelites who went from the enslaved to the enslavers in a few short generations, Christianity went from a small sect worshiping underground to avoid persecution from the empire to using its own liberation texts to justify the oppression of others. On a long enough timeline, the oppressed can become the oppressors.

It is important to note that while Christianity has oppressed and persecuted many individuals and communities, its practices and texts have also been a source of liberation. Martin Luther King, Jr. was a pastor, and his civil rights work was heavily influenced by his Christian values.

Christianity has everything to do with power—whether Christians are the victims of power structures or the powerful. We cannot understand Christianity without exploring both religious power and political power and a good place to begin is by looking at our language. Knowing the ways biblical and Christian language have been used to dehumanize, harm, torture, and enslave humans is the most important takeaway when thinking about the language of enslavement.

There are also curious ways enslavement language was used to make theological and practical points about those with whom Jesus was aligned during his lifetime. For example, Philippians 2:7–8 uses enslavement language when discussing Jesus: "but [he] emptied himself, taking the form of a slave . . . and became obedient to the point of death." Enslaved people were viewed as empty vessels without minds or agencies of their own. This emptiness allowed them, in the understanding of the culture, to be easily possessed either by demonic powers or by divine power.

For Jesus to empty himself like a slave can be seen as an alignment with the enslaved, with whom he had more in common with than with the Roman or Jewish elite. For Jesus to be filled with divine power, he had to become empty, just as enslaved people were presumed to be. Another way to think about this is that those filled with earthly power and ego were not empty enough to be filled with divine power.

Son of God

Jesus was not the first person to be called the Son of God. Humans have desired a God on earth in human form for a long time, which we can see in ancient Egyptian, Persian, Greek, and Roman myths. Pharaoh Thutmosis III, who lived from 1481 to 1425 BCE, proclaimed to be the son of the god in heaven. When Alexander the Great conquered Egypt in 332 BCE, he was crowned as Pharaoh and Son of God. In the Roman Empire in the year 40 BCE, Augustus visited the colonies in Gaul. A coin in Gaul was used to celebrate Augustus bringing a new era, and this coin read: "The divine Caesar—and the Son of God."[19] Roman emperors were considered to be the Son of God.

19. Ethelbert Stauffer, *Christ and the Caesars: Historical Sketches* (Eugene, OR: Wipf & Stock, 1952), 95.

We see the similarities in language used to describe political rulers and Jesus even more directly in the life of Julius Caesar. His reign had a policy of forgiveness and mercy, unlike those that came before him. The Roman people glorified Julius Caesar following his death, celebrating him as a slain deity. His great-nephew and adopted son, Augustus, became the first emperor of the Roman Empire. Augustus ruled Rome from 27 BCE to 14 CE, and like many rulers before him, he was considered the Son of God. Augustus was emperor when Jesus was born, and Tiberius, the stepson of Augustus, was emperor when Jesus died. During Jesus's lifetime living under Roman rule, emperors were commonly called Son of God.

In Christian history, it has been important to some authors and scribes that the Bible makes Jesus's identity clear. For example, the Gospel of Mark was the first written gospel. Many translations of Mark 1:1 say, "Son of God." The New Revised Standard Version of the Bible has a footnote clarifying that ancient authorities lack this phrase. To further complicate things, Son of God is not in the earliest manuscripts of Mark's gospel. Other biblical characters, especially King David (2 Samuel 7:14, Psalms 2:7, and Psalms 89:26), are referred to as "Son of God."

Identifying Jesus as the Son of God—whether by biblical writers, scribes, or later interpreters—was an anti-Caesar statement. Jesus was Lord, not the emperor. These are political statements. It was a bold way of saying that we don't worship the Roman Empire anymore. We don't bow down to oppressive power structures, but instead bow down to Jesus who has liberated us from this oppression.

Thief on the Cross

The gospels tell us that Jesus hung on his cross between two other men on crosses—two thieves. In Greek, they are called *lestai*, which can be also be translated as "bandits." Bandits were connected to the political movement taking place. They were not always thieves stealing for the sake of stealing, but members of bandit gangs acting out against a powerful political and religious system that had plenty of resources but refused to distribute these resources among all of its people.

We know the story of one of those thieves repenting in his last moments, gaining access to salvation and paradise. However, there is possibly more to the story given the political context of bandits in the Roman Empire. Perhaps they were angry with the established order on behalf of their loved ones and their communities. Perhaps they were operating outside of the law, because the law caused only hardship and the fight for survival. Operating outside of the law may have connected them to a political movement, giving them hope for a future without the oppression of the Jewish people.

These two thieves mocked Jesus as they were dying on their crosses. I imagine them in their last moments, the hysteria of these last hours of their lives. I wonder if they were full of regret or pride. I wonder if they saw their resistance efforts as useless, as yet another "messiah" hung between them dying. Perhaps this is why they mocked Jesus.

The bandits laughed and mocked Jesus along with those observing the crucifixion. This was not an unusual sight for the public. Bandits, traitors, and "messiahs" were often crucified. After seeing multiple supposed messiahs die on crosses, we might also have become jaded to the claim. Jesus was aware of this. Jesus, dying on his cross, says: "Father, forgive them; for they do not know what they are doing."

They didn't know. How could they? They hadn't heard Jesus's teachings. Many of these were Romans who benefited from the system.

Political movements that bring hope to the oppressed often fall on the deaf ears of those benefiting from the systems.

This political movement with its bandit gangs started before Jesus's birth and lasted beyond Jesus's death. Eventually it did manage to overthrow the Romans, though only for four years. The Jewish rebellion against Rome took place in 66 CE, about thirty years after Jesus's crucifixion. Jewish rebels had gained enough traction and energy from their fellow Jews, that they revolted against the Roman occupation of their city—and won! Four years later, in 70 CE, the Romans returned and violently took Jerusalem back. Jews were killed by the thousands, land and farms were destroyed, and Jerusalem was destroyed.

It's important to recall that the gospels were written after the Romans returned to control over the Jews and Jerusalem. The Gospel of Mark was written around 70–71 CE; the Gospel of Matthew and the Gospel of Luke were written around 99–100 CE; and the Gospel of John was written between 100 and 120 CE. There were many reasons to disassociate Jesus, their Messiah, from the political movement that ended in such violence and Jewish bloodshed. Instead of telling the story of Jesus as part of a political movement against the Romans, they told his story in a way the Romans could accept—as they later did when Christianity and Rome merged a few centuries later.

This context helps us see the thief on the cross who asks Jesus to remember him as somebody aligned against the same Roman system Jesus spoke out against. When Jesus told him he would be with him in paradise, perhaps this was Jesus acknowledging the common injustice that both he and the thief experienced. Although Jesus and this bandit resisted the empire with different efforts and ethics, this may have been Jesus recognizing the thief's resistance efforts.

◇◇◇

Time

Two Greek words are translated into English as time—*chronos* and *kairos*. *Chronos*, as in chronology, has to do with the linear sequence of events. This is the version of time Westerners think of most often. *Kairos*, which is used nearly twice as often as *chronos* in the Bible, refers to something significant happening when the time is right. Sometimes *kairos* is translated as "seasonal" or "in God's time." *Kairos* does not refer to a perceived date on the calendar or time on a clock, but instead refers to a point in time when conditions are right for a significant event to unfold.

For example, farmers do not have a date and time to harvest; harvesting occurs when the time is right, which is conditional based on sunlight, rain, soil, and other factors beyond complete human control. Similarly, many Jewish people were waiting for a messiah when the "fullness of the time came" (Galatians 4:4), as Paul says. This was not an expected point in time, but instead a time when conditions were right for a messiah to emerge.

Time in Western culture is usually discussed, viewed, and experienced chronologically, a tendency that has been fostered by the Industrial Revolution. As the expression goes, "time is money." The dictum has become so dominant that the Institute of Standards and Technology, part of the U.S. Department of Commerce, is responsible for maintaining official time in the United States. The connection between time and the economy is strong

Time and power in Western cultures, especially the United States, saturate all aspects of our lives. We value traits like efficiency and timeliness, but these are not universal values, nor have they been throughout history. Biblical cultures had different understandings of time, and Western Christians can misread biblical texts if we project our own understandings of time onto our interpretations of the Bible.

Turn the Other Cheek

"Turn the other cheek" has become a common saying, even outside of the church, and is often understood to mean responding to offense without retaliation. Many people think Jesus meant to avoid conflict, but this interpretation can be used to allow oneself to be taken advantage of or to allow abuse. However, Jesus is telling his followers something else when he says turn the other cheek.

We often imagine only two responses to violence: revenge or avoidance. But there is a third, creative way to respond to violence and abuses of power. To understand the point of the turn the other cheek concept, we must first drop into Jewish culture and the society of Jesus's time.

In Matthew 5:38–41, Jesus is rejecting the teaching of "eye for an eye and tooth for a tooth" and instead instructing his followers to resist an evildoer: turning the other cheek if struck on the right cheek, giving your cloak should someone take your coat, and going an extra mile when required to go one mile. This text is from the Sermon on the Mount. Jesus lived by Jewish law and knew the Hebrew Bible well. Exodus and Leviticus have much to say about retributive action, and Jesus is drawing from these texts in his Sermon on the Mount.

Jesus wasn't interested in revenge as a means to take power from the powerful. He wasn't interested in maintaining the cycle of abusive power and violence. He also wasn't interested in submitting to the powers that be. Jesus was teaching a new way of living. He was telling his audience to go above and beyond the common understanding of the law and what was fair to flip power on its head, to neutralize the power structures that be.

Let's break it down line by line.

"An eye for an eye and a tooth for a tooth":

The Law of Moses uses this phrase. It appears in Exodus 21:23–25, Leviticus 24:19–20, and Deuteronomy 19:21. Outside the Law of Moses, Roman law has the "law of equals" and a similar expectation appears in the ancient Babylonian Code of Hammurabi. But this line has been abused. Its original intent was to limit the powers of the civil government to punish people. When governments were sentencing people to death for petty crimes, these laws, including the phrase we find in Hebrew scripture, were intended to limit punishments. In essence, it was stating that the punishment should match the crime, and not go beyond.

"Do not resist an evildoer":

To resist those who have power over us is to oppose and defy them. Resistance is a normal human response to evil, but Jesus does not teach his followers to respond in this way, because it often only serves to escalate abuse and violence. Jesus doesn't teach us to ignore and enable, but instead has a different idea about how to handle oppressive power structures.

Jesus is teaching people to go beyond resistance and into something new—something more creative and permanent, and something that stops retribution in its tracks. He goes on to give examples of this creative response to power by telling his followers to turn the other cheek.

"If anyone strikes you on the right cheek, turn the other also":

In the first century, the right hand was the hand of power. The right hand was used, among other things, to hit people. The left hand was used for bodily functions, like cleaning yourself after a bowel movement. To slap somebody on the right cheek with their right hand would be a backhanded slap. This kind of slap was viewed as dismissive and humiliating in nature. Lamentations 3:30 discusses giving one's cheek to a smiter as an insult. Paul discusses the humiliation of a strike on the face in 2 Corinthians 11:20.

In the first century, there were two ways to hit someone: a punch or a slap with the back of the hand. Equals were punched; subordinates were slapped. Try this now. Face another person. Hold up your right fist and pretend to punch them on the right cheek. It is awkward, almost impossible. Jesus says, "if anyone strikes you on the right cheek." He specifically states that this is a strike, not a punch. That strike or slap is a public statement of social hierarchy.

If somebody slaps your right cheek, turn the other cheek. In turning your left cheek to them, you are forcing them to punch you instead of slap you, the acknowledgement of social equality.

"If anyone wants to sue you and take your coat, give your cloak as well":

In the first century, Jews paid taxes to the Roman Empire, to the Temple, and to the Herodians, the violent local government. Under this triple taxation, Jewish families were losing their land, animals, and crops. If a person was deep in debt, their coat would be taken as payment. This would be done publicly at the city gate. Jesus was saying if somebody is trying to take advantage of you and to humiliate you, give them everything. Literally, give them the clothes off your back.

Jesus would have been familiar with Exodus 22:26–27: "If you take your neighbor's cloak as a pledge, return it by sunset, because that cloak is the only covering your neighbor has. What else can they sleep in? When they cry out to me, I will hear, for I am compassionate." Jesus is expanding on this text when he says to give your cloak as well.

The Law of Moses states that no one can take and keep your cloak. Jesus was telling people to use this law to neutralize power. In our lives today, it is shameful to be naked. However, the opposite was true in Jesus's time. The person who saw the naked one was more ashamed than the person who was naked. To see nakedness was more shameful than to be naked. By suggesting that when one's coat was taken, to also give the cloak was to force the person in power to both break the law by taking your cloak and to see you naked, causing them public shame.

Jesus was a funny and creative guy. And he just keeps adding to the suggestions so his audience fully understands his point.

"If anyone forces you to go one mile, go also the second mile":

We have all heard the expression, "go the extra mile." It is usually said to encourage harder work or extra effort. That is not exactly what Jesus was saying, though.

In the occupied land of Israel there was no access to horses or other strong animals, so people had to walk and carry equipment. In Jesus's time, the law allowed Roman soldiers to force any Jew to carry the soldier's equipment up to one mile. If you were on your way to work or outside of your home, a Roman soldier was allowed to stop you and make you carry their pack for one mile.

Jesus was telling people to walk two miles instead. Literally, go the extra mile. This, in turn, forced the Roman soldier to break the law. The soldier is now in danger of serious punishment. And the Romans didn't mess around when it came to punishments.

We see this law in practice at Jesus's crucifixion. Matthew 27:32 tells readers that a man was forced to carry Jesus's cross. Mark 15:21 similarly says that a passer-by carried Jesus's cross. Luke 23:26 references this, too, by saying that they seized a man and made him carry the cross behind Jesus.

In context, it becomes obvious that this passage is not saying that we should allow ourselves to be abused and taken advantage of. To turn our cheek is not to ignore evil or avoid conflict, but to respond creatively to destructive power dynamics without participating in the oppressive system. To give the cloak off our back is not to live a completely selfless and giving life, but to give the shame back to the one abusing their power without violence. To go the extra mile creates a possible vulnerability for one using their position of authority.

Jesus was telling his followers not to return evil for evil. Instead, Jesus creatively combatted corrupt authority. Jesus taught that we should disarm our enemies rather than inflict revenge on them. Power should be neutralized, not conquered.

Jesus was using common cultural understandings of the day to demonstrate the way he wanted people to live their lives. He was teaching people that the idea of power is a lie. Those at the top are vulnerable, too. The systems that keep some people at the top and others at the bottom are all a house of cards. They can be easily manipulated and flipped on their heads by turning the other cheek. Seemingly powerful, they are instead weak and temporary.

Virgin

The Christian story we have inherited says that Jesus was born to a virgin. The Septuagint, the Greek translation of the Hebrew Bible, uses the Greek word *parthenos*, often translated as "virgin," to describe the woman who will birth Immanuel. *Parthenos* is related to the Parthenon, the Greek temple dedicated to Athena, the virgin goddess. *Parthenos* is used to describe non-virgins in the Bible. For example, in Genesis 34:3, Dinah is described as a *parthenos* after just having sexual intercourse.

The Hebrew uses the word *'almah*, which does not imply virginity but instead means "young, unmarried girl." Virginity entered the story with the translation from Hebrew to Greek somewhere around 285–247 BCE. This translation choice has had a long-lasting impact on Christianity. Isaiah 7:14 is often used to prove that the Messiah must be born of a virgin, but understanding the translation from Hebrew to Greek negates this. In fact, some Christians burned copies of the 1952 Revised

Standard Version for its accurate translation of ʻalmah as "young woman" instead of "virgin." It's also important to note that Judaism does not understand this text as a prophecy that the Messiah's mother was a virgin.

Mary's virginity is still a part of the story we have inherited and continues to be debated among theologians and historians. Some Christians believe in Mary's perpetual virginity, but the gospels state that Jesus had brothers and sisters. Christian apologists have attempted to stretch this understanding to mean cousins, but this is unconvincing.

A woman's virginity in antiquity typically meant the lack of a husband. To be considered a virgin in a time when virginity was so closely connected to the construct of marriage can refer to a woman who belongs to herself, rather than a woman who belongs to a man. Perhaps a woman has enough wealth and resources to survive without a man, a difficult and unusual thing at that time. To be a virgin may be another way to say a woman is independent.

Three women are often a focus in Christianity: Mary the mother of Jesus, Mary Magdalene, and Eve. Tropes have been created of the three by referring to them as Mary the virgin, Mary the previously demon-possessed, and Eve the sinner. These are slim pickings when it comes to the female tropes available to Christian women. Mary Magdalene and Eve, of course, have been interpreted in our patriarchal world to have been in close alignment with the devil. On the other hand, identifying with Mary the mother of Jesus meant virginity.

During the Middle Ages, the status of virgin could be an empowering option for women. To have a role model within the Christian narrative who was a virgin implied that there was a noble path forward that did not involve marriage or motherhood. To remain a virgin and join a convent provided another more liberating option for many women.

Mary's virgin status is something we will likely continue to debate. For me, it does not make or break the story. Instead, understanding people's strong desire to understand Mary as remaining a virgin is a glimpse into the various tropes about women: we are either sexually pure, or we are demon possessed or aligned with the devil. Seeing virginity as potential for liberation creates new possibilities. Women are not characters who need to live up to an ideal. Mary, virgin or not, was a person—a person who contributed to one of the biggest shifts in human history.

Whore of Babylon

A LEADER OF VARIOUS EARLY JESUS COMMUNITIES named John was exiled to the Greek island of Patmos, likely by Emperor Domitian. In exile, he wrote his communities a letter we now call the Revelation of John. John wrote to these specific communities using many images and symbols they would have understood. Revelation has its own cultural context situated in the late first century. John of Patmos was writing to seven specific communities, and all of these communities were a part of the Roman Empire. One of the popular phrases and images John uses is the great whore, or the whore of Babylon (Revelation 17).

John discusses a whore, but not-so-subtly hints to his audience who this whore is by naming her Babylon the great (Revelation 18:5) and saying she is on seven hills (Revelation 17:9). The Babylonians destroyed the First Temple, so the Romans, who destroyed the Second Temple, were often called Babylon. The seven hills were notably pointing to Rome, which is known as the city built on seven hills. Clearly, the whore is a reference to Rome and the Roman Empire. Interestingly, this is not the only place a city is depicted as a female prostitute in the Bible. Tyre and Nineveh are also described this way (Nahum 3:4, Isaiah 23:16–7).

This whore, or prostitute, is described as being clothed in purple and scarlet. Purple dye was very expensive to make and access. Additionally, she is said to have gold, jewels, and pearls. John is pointing to Rome's excessive wealth.

The image of a prostitute is used because John is likening sexual promiscuity to religious infidelity, as if collaborating with the Romans is similar to cheating on God. Painting Rome as a whore makes John's point clear to his audience: Rome is seductive, but you must not be tempted by the riches and power they offer.

The image of the whore of Babylon, although problematic for its sexist use of women's sexuality, must be situated in its historical and cultural context to understand that John is speaking about the evils of the Roman Empire throughout Revelation. His repeated references to sexual infidelity are his way of referencing the idolatrous act of betraying God to collaborate with the Romans.

This is not a text predicting the future or a checklist of things that must occur before the second coming of Jesus or the end of the world as we know it. Reading the Bible, and specifically Revelation, this way results in some Christians assuming war and violence is necessary to fulfill John of Patmos's prophetic vision. This theological stance can make us passive to the suffering of others and can halt needed humanitarian action. The way we read the Bible has real-life implications. John of Patmos is writing to his communities to remind them that Rome is the enemy and they need to stay loyal to Jesus, no matter the cost. Collaborating with Rome, or the whore of Babylon, was idolatrous.

YHWH

God tells Moses that God's name is *YHWH.* Ancient Hebrew was written without vowels, so when we try to pronounce *YHWH* we find ourselves breathing in and out, making the sound of breath. Many make connections between this name for God and the breath of life.

For much of this history, *YHWH* was seen as too sacred to say out loud, so Jews did not say it or even write it. In many versions of the Bible, LORD is written in all caps to draw the reader's attention to the fact that something interesting was happening with this word. LORD may appear in the Hebrew Bible in place of *YHWH.* Instead of saying the sacred name of *YHWH*, the people said *Adonai*, which means "the Lord." Some refused to even say *Adonai*, instead saying *ha-Shem*, meaning "the Name." This practice continues among some Jews today.

Vowels were added to the Hebrew language of the Bible during the Middle Ages, and many English speakers pronounce *YHWH* now as "Yahweh." Sometimes we see it mispronounced as Jehovah. Nevertheless, what we do know about the sacred name *YHWH* is that it is in the verb form "to be." Therefore, God told Moses that God is a verb rather than a noun.

Zealots

During Jesus's life, there were several Jewish sects, among them the Pharisees, the Sadducees, the Herodians, the Essenes, and the Zealots. The Zealots were not a formalized sect or party until about 66 CE, decades after Jesus was killed. However, the Zealot ideology existed during his time and the roots of the Zealots were forming during his lifetime. For example, Simon the Zealot held these ideological views, but the Zealots as such did not officially exist yet.

The Zealots were a Jewish political movement that worked to overthrow Roman rule at all costs. They were a radical group of anti-Roman revolutionaries who believed God should rule Israel, not the Roman Empire. They were known for their violent and militaristic resistance to Roman control. They appeared at the beginning of the First Jewish–Roman War.

In the Septuagint and New Testament, the Greek word *zēlos*, or zeal, can mean righteous passion or destructive envy, depending on the context. In this sense, both John the Baptist and Jesus of Nazareth can be considered zealous. They both speak passionately about reform. However, to be zealous during this time was not the same as belonging to the Zealots. Some scholars, like Reza Aslan,[20] argue that Jesus may have been a formal Zealot. However, this view is not widely accepted.

We often think of Judaism during Jesus's time as having a unified vision and interpretation of the faith, but this is untrue. Like Christianity, there were many variants of Judaism—each with their own sets of beliefs, practices, and political alignment.

20. Reza Aslan, *Zealot: The Life and Times of Jesus of Nazareth* (New York: Random House, 2013).

CHURCH LANGUAGE

Christianity extends beyond the Bible. It always has. In fact, there are no Christians in the Bible. The earliest communities of Jesus followers did not consider themselves to be "Christians." Christianity as a community organized around a shared set of beliefs did not exist until a few centuries after Jesus was killed by the Roman Empire. Instead, there were regional communities that began to gather and appeared to have some components of their identity that were connected to Jesus. However, these gatherings of people had very little uniformity in their theological identity. There is little evidence to support the idea that there was a unified understanding of who Jesus was and who Jesus's followers were in the first two hundred years after Jesus's crucifixion. The understandings of Jesus were being debated and constructed primarily through conversation and other oral traditions. Reading, which was always communal, played a small role in early Jesus communities.

Most early Jesus communities were small groups that came together to share food and discuss their lives in a posture of compassion and support—a ritual that opposed the "support" of the Roman Empire, which deemed itself the savior of those they conquered. Rome did use its powerful militia to protect those within the empire from the violent pirates who would attack the people of Roman-occupied lands. However, governmental protection has a frequent companion of governmental oppression. Many within the empire had their livelihoods and their cultural habits restricted; people were going without jobs, homes, and food. Small Jesus communities acted as families and units of protection and provision.

The associations of the anointed—or early communities of Jesus followers—were diverse. Some were a space for oppressed voices to be heard. Women, the enslaved, and day laborers were present here, and there is evidence that they had voices and positions of power in these spaces, unlike elsewhere across the empire. However, we cannot glorify the earliest Jesus communities as consistently equitable. Women sometimes had high status within these groups, while at other times they were silenced. Enslaved people may have been forced into membership within these Jesus associations. They were considered extensions and subordinate members of their households, and it was common for entire households to become a part of a Jesus community (Acts 16:15, Acts 16:33, and 1 Corinthians 1:16). There is no way of knowing whether enslaved participants in the Jesus communities chose to identify with these associations.

Eventually, the movement called Christianity took form, but the term "Christian" was not originally a name that believers adopted for themselves. More often in the first two centuries, *Christianos* (Greek for Christ-follower) was a term that nonbelievers used to describe Jesus communities. *Christian* is a transliteration of the original Greek. The main root of this word, *christos*, comes from the Hebrew word *messiah*, meaning "anointed with oil." In Israel, this was a direct reference to kings, prophets, and priests who were anointed with oil when they took on their new identity as a leader. The suffix *-ian* means "belongs to the party of." Therefore, to be a Christian means to belong to the party of the Anointed One.

To Rome, the emperor was the anointed one. To belong to a party that did not claim the emperor as the anointed one, or messiah, was treason. Christ followers, *Christianos*, clearly denied to acknowledge the emperor as the anointed one. This meaning becomes less clear when the Greek word becomes a Latin word, however. In Latin, "to be anointed or oiled" would have been *unctus*, which had no linguistic connection to *christianos*. Christians living under Roman rule were called *Christianus*, transliterated from the Greek. Many of our English Bibles have been translated from the Latin Vulgate, taking us one step further from that original Greek word and its connotation of being dangerously opposed to the oppressive political powers anointed into their leadership roles.

The New Testament contains about 138,000 words, depending on the translation, and *christianos* is found only three times among these tens of thousands of words. It is not found in any four of the canonical gospels or Paul's letters. It is found in Acts of the Apostles 11:25–26, Acts of the Apostles 26:27–29, and 1 Peter 4:14–16. Acts of the Apostles is widely agreed to have been written after 125 CE and 1 Peter after 150 CE. These three biblical texts from Acts of the Apostles and 1 Peter are read very differently when we understand that Christianity did not yet exist as a religion separate from those who followed the God of Israel. Instead of reading these texts as pointing to the Christian religion, we must read them as pointing to "the party of the Anointed One." To claim membership in this party is to be in direct opposition of the Roman Empire—a dangerous and life-threatening stance to take.

Christianity became a formal religion in the early fourth century CE when the Roman emperor Constantine embraced and formalized it.

While tradition states that Constantine was genuinely transformed by Christ, there is evidence that Constantine's support of Jesus followers was politically opportunistic.[21] However, his support led to the legalization of Christianity and the official merger of church and political power.

Interestingly, while the term "Christian" began as a bureaucratic and pejorative way for the Roman Empire to identify these small groups of Jesus followers, ultimately Jesus followers reclaimed the term as their own. This linguistic process of reappropriation or reclamation of words across cultures is how identity and language work. We see this reclamation regularly in Christian history. "Protestant" began as a derogatory term, but now about a billion people identify proudly as Protestant. Similarly, members of the Religious Society of Friends were rudely called "Quakers," but they later reclaimed the term for themselves.

Reappropriation or reclamation is an empowering use of language. In contemporary society, examples abound. Black Americans were, and continue to be, called the n-word by white Americans—a word so pejorative in nature that many don't speak it or even spell it out in its entirety. Many Black communities have reclaimed this word as their own, and use a modified form within their communities. Similarly, women have a long history of being called "bitches," yet many now use this word casually when talking with friends. *Queer* began as a word for "strange" and was used to offend members of LGBT communities, but now refers to any individual or community not heterosexual or cisgender. Pride in one's identity can reform language and resist the power that has been previously leveraged through language. The same word can be offensive or empowering, depending on who is speaking and the context. Language is stretchy and complex in this way.

21. Dana L. Robert, *Christian Mission: How Christianity Became a World Religion* (Hoboken, NJ: Wiley-Blackwell, 2009), 16–18.

The same is true for Christians. Language has everything to do with identity, and how we name ourselves exposes our identity. As those small early gatherings began to gain power in the face of longstanding oppression, they eventually reclaimed the word Christian. The development of Christians calling themselves "church" is an extension and expansion of biblical language. The Greek word *ekklesia* is often translated as "church." The root *ek* means "out of" and *kaleo* means "to call," so *ekklesia* means "called out" or "called together." In ancient Greek society, *ekklesia* did not refer to a spiritual community but to a gathering of citizens for political purposes. *Ekklesia* in the New Testament described the assembly or gathering of Jesus followers, and eventually it evolved to mean a spiritual community. The word *ekklesia* did not refer to a building, but to the people. In other words, a church is the congregation, not the building in which the congregation gathers.

Israelites gathered together for worship were typically called a "synagogue" in the first two centuries CE. *Synagogue* means "to bring together," and it is a transliteration of the Greek word for "meeting." In the first two centuries, a synagogue was not a specific place or building, but instead a group or gathering. Additionally, it was not a term exclusive to Jewish associations; this term was also used for associations of barbers and shippers who honored the sea god Poseidon.[22] Synagogues included both Jewish people and early Jesus followers, both of whom were considered people of Israel, whether their ancestors were Israelites or not.

Much of the language of early Jesus communities is preserved in the creeds many liturgical churches continue to use today. For example, the Nicene Creed, formulated at the Councils of Nicaea (325 CE) and

22. Erin K. Vearncombe, Bernard Brandon Scott, and Hal Taussig. *After Jesus Before Christianity: A Historical Exploration of the First Two Centuries of Jesus Movements* (New York: HarperOne, 2021), 168.

Constantinople (381 CE), is a detailed statement of belief many denominations continue to profess and affirm. Official creeds upheld by many churches today include the Apostles' Creed, Nicene Creed, and Athanasian Creed. Many words and phrases found in the major Christian creeds do not appear in the Bible in the exact form used in the creeds. Many council debates used words and phrases outside of the Bible to formulate church doctrine.

For example, the Bible does not use the word *catholic*, meaning "universal," to describe the Church, but the Apostles' Creed and Nicene Creed state, "I believe in one holy, catholic, and apostolic Church." Similarly, the creeds use the word *substance* to describe the divine nature of Christ as being of the same substance as the Father, but this term does not appear in the Bible. The word *Trinity* is not found in the Bible. While the concept of God as Father, Son, and Holy Spirit is found in Scripture, the word *Trinity* itself is not biblical. The church has a long history of using language outside of the Bible to form doctrine and belief.

In the mid-nineteenth century, Christianity felt itself to be in opposition to culture's growing sense of reason, rationalism, and science. To combat this, Catholics declared the Pope as "infallible" and many Protestants deemed the Bible as "inerrant." Every group had their authoritative figures. The belief that the Bible contains solely literal and historical truths is a relatively new Christian belief.

In Hebrew, the phrase "Word of God" is *Davar Elohim*. This phrase refers to the communication from God to humans and is often used in reference to the prophets. In the New Testament, John's Gospel opens with "In the beginning was the Word." This use of "Word" does not mean words of the Bible. "Word" here is a translation of the Greek word *Logos*, used to describe Jesus as the divine expression of God. *Logos* is also the root from which we get the word *logic*, which refers to reasoning or wisdom. We can see how Word, Christ, and wisdom intertwine in the identity of Jesus as defined in the Bible. Interestingly, wisdom is feminine in the original languages of the Bible and sometimes referred to as *Sophia*, from its Greek root.

Exploring liturgical history also reveals the ways "Word of God" has gained layers of meaning throughout time. In many churches today, after a biblical text is read, the reader and congregation say, "The Word of the Lord . . . Thanks be to God." In the mid-twentieth century, many churches began to use the pattern to emphasize the divine authority and significance of scripture. This shift was influenced by liturgical reforms such as in the Second Vatican Council for Roman Catholics and the 1979 Book of Common Prayer for Episcopalians.

Before the liturgical reforms of the Second Vatican Council (1962–1965), the Roman Catholic Church followed a one-year pattern of readings called the Common Lectionary. After Vatican II and the resultant liturgical changes across Christian denominations, a three-year Revised Common Lectionary began to be widely used. Churches using the Revised Common Lectionary typically hear four readings in worship—an Old Testament reading, a Psalm, an epistle, and a Gospel reading. With this revised lectionary, a renewed emphasis correlating the Old Testament lesson with the epistle and Gospel was strengthened by responding to the Old Testament and epistle with "The Word of the Lord." This shift to "The Word of the Lord" following Old Testament readings brought attention to the belief that the God of the Old Testament is the God of the New Testament, seeing the through-line of divinity throughout the Old and New Testaments.

Scripture, whether we comfortably call it the "Word of God" or not, is full of human experiences of God. Referring to scripture as the "Word of the Lord" is not stating that scripture is infallible or that it cannot be critiqued and wrestled with. On the contrary, if scripture is to be viewed as containing divine presence and truths, it must be wrestled with. Jacob was renamed *Israel*, which means "one who wrestles with God." To be God's people means to wrestle with and even struggle with God. Wrestling with how God is depicted in the Bible is messy, and the only way to engage with it is to enter the mess. That's what Jesus the Christ, who is the actual Word of God for Christians, did—willingly entered the messiness of the human experience.

Christianity is formed from the riches of both church tradition and biblical texts. Some language can be found directly in the Bible, while some words are used to articulate theological concepts and church practices. Some church language is contained within the Bible, and yet some church language extends beyond the biblical tradition. Church tradition, and therefore "church language," often interprets the biblical text as it has been shaped through the centuries to include the seasons, rituals, customs, and rites of the Church.

Advent

The Advent season has made its way into the Christian liturgical calendar as the time before Christmas when we await the birth of Jesus. The word *advent* is derived from the Latin word *adventus*, meaning "coming" or "arrival," and it has imperial roots. The desire for God to become human has existed for many millennia. In 31 BCE, Gaius Octavius, who was the adopted son of Julius Caesar and later known as Augustus, defeated Antony and Cleopatra in the Battle of Actium, ultimately making him the first emperor of the Roman Empire. Virgil's poem *Aeneid* helped mythologize Augustus and his role in forming the empire, and he uses the word *adventus* to refer to Augustus. In the year 17 BCE, Augustus implemented a twelve-day Advent celebration in his name, hence the "twelve days of Christmas" song many are familiar with. The Roman emperor was considered to be the heavenly savior of the people, and emperors had coins made to commemorate their advent, or arrival. In the year 67 CE, Nero had coins inscribed with "Adventus Augusti," meaning "the Arrival of the August One." Emperor Hadrian had coins commemorating his journey through his empire that bore the words "Adventus Augusti" and images of children carrying palms to welcome the emperor.

Many emperors were believed to be the savior, so many advents were celebrated and commemorated. It is estimated that the third century CE had over 60 Roman emperors, many who were ruling unofficially in fractions of the empire. There were only so many times a person could celebrate the arrival of someone who was supposed to save people from their hardships before they lost trust in the system. Constantine the Great seemed to grasp this swaying trust, and with his reign Christianity was formally recognized as a religion. Jesus of Nazareth was deemed the one who saves. The understandings of advent that were used to discuss the arrival of emperors were transferred to Jesus.

One focus of Epiphany was Jesus's baptism in the Jordan River, and in the early church, Advent was a season of baptismal preparation. In the fourth and fifth centuries in the Western Church, Advent was focused on preparing for the second coming of Christ and the coming Kingdom of God, rather than on the remembrance of the birth of Jesus. Over time, the liturgical season of Advent emphasized the awaiting of Jesus's birth.

The Church's liturgical year begins with the season of Advent, which leads to Christmas. While some Christian traditions celebrate a seven-week Advent season, it is more common currently to celebrate a four-week Advent. The seven weeks of Advent is observed primarily in Eastern Christian traditions and lasts forty days, or about seven weeks. In both the West and the East, Christian observances of Advent are about waiting, fasting, praying, and preparing. The Western Church standardized a four week Advent season under Pope Gregory I in the sixth century, and the Eastern Church committed to longer periods of fasting, praying, and preparation during the Advent season.

In Roman Catholic, Lutheran, Anglican, and many other Protestant denominations, Advent begins four Sundays before Christmas and ends at Christmas Eve. This season is often commemorated by the candles of the Advent wreath, which symbolize Jesus's birth as the arrival of light in the world. Four candles are used, holding a variety of symbolic meanings. Some churches include a taller candle in the middle, called a Christ candle, which is lit on Christmas Eve.

The Advent season has imperial roots. Despite the evolution of Advent throughout the centuries, the core of Advent is about the arrival and reign of a savior. For Christians, this savior is Jesus the Christ. Each year, our church year begins by awaiting the arrival of Christ.

American Flag

Symbols are a type of language. Spoken or written language helps us communicate, and symbols are another form of communication. Just as the cross has become a universal symbol of Christianity, the flag is the symbol of the United States of America. Although some churches do include a flag in their nave or worship space, the flag and the cross do not hold hands. In fact, the cross holds the flag accountable for domination and oppression. Similarly, reciting the Pledge of Allegiance at a Christian worship service echoes pledging Caesar as King, not Christ.

The Flag Code (United States Statutes at Large, Seventy-seventh Congress, Second Session 1942, Volume 56—Part 1, Public Laws) states in Section 3 (k): "When displayed from a staff in a church or public auditorium, the [American] flag should occupy the position of honor and be placed at the clergyman's or speaker's right as he faces the congregation or audience. Any other flag so displayed in the chancel or on the platform should be placed to the clergyman's or speaker's left as he faces the congregation or audience. But when the flag is displayed from a staff in a church or public auditorium elsewhere than in the chancel or on the platform, it shall be placed in the position of honor at the right of the congregation or audience as they face the chancel or platform. Any other flag so displayed should be placed on the left of the congregation or audience as they face the chancel or platform."

The Flag Code and Christianity both signify placement on the right as the place of honor. When we place the American flag on the right side in our worship, we are stating the flag is greater than Christ—a heresy for any Christian. If we place the American flag somewhere other than the right, we are breaking the Flag Code.

When Herod rebuilt the Temple in Jerusalem, he placed a golden eagle over the main portal of the Temple. A golden eagle was the symbol of Roman domination, and the Romans conquered the Israelites and ruled over them. The Temple was the central place of Jewish worship and identity, so placing a Roman symbol here was a statement about who had power in this space. This is not entirely different than the placement of the American flag in Christian worship spaces. The symbols in our worship spaces communicate where we place our power.

Baptism

Baptism in Greek is *baptizo*, which did not originally refer to a religious practice. Instead, it simply meant "bathing" or "dipping." A *baptizo* was simply a bath people took. The practice of baptisms did not begin as a religious or Christian practice. There were many public baths in the Mediterranean people used to cleanse themselves, both physically and morally. The idea behind this practice was once a person had bathed, they could re-enter the community with a sense of cleanliness and renewal. This was separate from any particular religious ceremony or ritual. Public baths were a common part of life.

John the Baptist is known for baptizing people in the Jordan River. John the Baptist—or John the Bather—was extending the common Roman practice of bathing away physical and moral filth. However, there is an important differentiation about what John was doing. He was not necessarily bathing or baptizing people into the faith governed by the God of Israel. Instead, he was bathing people from their moral failings related to collaborating with the Roman Empire. Many Israelites were benefiting from the oppressive Roman system for their own personal gains. These public bathings were cleansing people of their collaboration with Rome so they could come back into the fold of Jewish life with a sense of renewed cleanliness. This was a part of the Jewish rebellion against the Roman Empire. John was baptizing people into the community of Jewish resistance.

John the Baptist was serious about avoiding any kind of collaboration with the Roman system of oppression. Romans built public baths around the Temple in Jerusalem, a bold display of power. John the Baptist refused to bathe people in Roman-made baths, so he used bodies of water, like the Jordan River, outside of Jerusalem. People had to walk several days to get to the Jordan River, demonstrating the commitment of John and others in distancing themselves from the Roman way of doing things.

Acts of the Apostles refers to these common bathings taking place outside of Israel, but baptisms as a religious or Christian practice did not exist during Jesus's life or in the earliest Jesus communities following his life. They picked up this meaning later. Transliterated, *baptism* became a new word able to take on new meaning in a religious context. It wasn't until after the Bar Kokhba War of 132–136 CE, a Jewish rebellion against the Romans, when the practice of baptism began to be less associated with rebellion against the Romans. Eventually, the practice of baptism became more associated with being cleansed into communities of Jesus followers, although it is not clear historically how and when this association took place.

There are disagreements among Christians about who can be baptized, when they can be baptized, who can do the baptizing, how many times a person can or should be baptized, and the overall meaning of baptism. A few things are clear about the origins of baptism: Baptism has roots related to both resisting oppressive systems and being cleansed into a community.

Baptism became a sacrament, which in ancient times was understood as an oath of allegiance to the emperor by a soldier, which was made visible by branding the soldier's arm or forehead. When someone is baptized, a part of the rite includes anointing them with oil on the forehead in the sign of the cross, called *christening*. In christening, we see the preservation of the original meaning of Christian to mean "party of the anointed," by literally anointing someone with oil into the community. *Christ* means "anointed one," and Jesus being titled the Christ is in direct opposition to the kings and emperors who were anointed upon their reign. When we are baptized and anointed into the community, we take a sacramental mark on our forehead demonstrating our oath to Christ. This can be seen as an anti-imperial sentiment.

Baptism is not simply a mark on an individual's life. Baptism is a communal ritual. This is how a new and better world is created—by freely giving membership into a community that refuses to hold hands with oppressive power. This kind of resistance can only be maintained with a community.

Belief

Belief means to have confidence in someone, and it comes into English from the Germanic word *glauben. Glauben* is related to the Indo-European root *lubh*, which is the root for our English word *love*. The Old English *be loaf* means "to hold dear," making the connection between *believe* and *beloved*. To believe is to hold someone dear.

To believe in something is to love it and prefer it over something or someone else. To believe in something or someone is more about the action of the person doing the believing than the qualities of the object being believed. If somebody says, "I believe in you," they are not acknowledging that you exist, but instead that they view you with a certain favor or love. To believe is to accept and have faith in what cannot be proven or verified. In fact, faith comes from the Latin word *fidere*, which means "to trust." We cannot believe in something, but on it, as we see in the King James Version that says "believe on the Lord Jesus Christ" (Acts 16:31). If we believe on, rather than believe in, it is like something we lean on for foundation.

Born Again

The phrase "born again" has its roots primarily in Christianity, and its meaning has evolved over time. The Greek phrase *gennēthē anōthen* can be found in John 3:3. *Gennēthē* means "to be born." *Anōthen* can mean either "from above" or "again." There are differing translations of John 3:3.

In this passage, Jesus is speaking to Nicodemus, who is a Pharisee and therefore among the religious elite Jesus speaks out against. In the

New King James Version, Jesus says, "Most assuredly, I say to you, unless one is born again, he cannot see the kingdom of God." In the New Revised Standard Version, on the other hand, Jesus says, "Very truly, I tell you, no one can see the kingdom of God without being born from above." Many consider "born from above" as a more accurate translation than "born again."[23] Either way, Nicodemus interprets Jesus's words as meaning a literal birth and even questions how one would return to their mother's womb. Jesus clarifies by saying one must be born anew of water and Spirit.

The double meaning of the Greek word *anōthen* as both "again" and "from above" creates this theological debate. Early Christians understood being born again as a spiritual rebirth. Church fathers like Origen and Augustine connected being born again to the sacrament of baptism, marking a transformation into the Christian faith. During the Protestant Reformation, Martin Luther and John Calvin emphasized spiritual rebirth through grace rather than works. A "born again Christian" is an identity marker that has made its way into dominant conservative discourse.

Born again theology, which centralizes the moment a decision is made to accept Jesus, continues to be prominent in American evangelical culture. Some Christians believe that becoming Christian is an individual decision. Debating the phrase "born again" touches on an ongoing debate that extends beyond Christianity about human choice and agency. This debate continues in theology, philosophy, psychology, and politics. Augustine argued that humans could only be saved by God's grace, while Pelagius said people make good choices on their own. Some Christians emphasize God's grace for salvation, while others believe free will and personal choice are necessary for salvation. John Locke argued that humans are

23. Marcus J. Borg, *Speaking Christian: Why Christian Words Have Lost Their Power and How They Can Be Restored* (New York: HarperCollins Publishers, 2011), 167.

born as a blank slate and their lives can be shaped through education and choice. The idea of autonomy and personal agency has become an American virtue, ultimately influencing many expressions of Christianity.

The way we understand decisions is connected to our language. In English, we *make* a decision. However, in languages like Spanish, French, and Italian, decisions are something you *take*, like a train you take to journey somewhere. Linguistically, when decisions are described as being taken, they carry the implication of accessing or receiving something already in existence. However, when decisions are discussed as something we make, it is understood that our choices are produced and created by us alone. The phrase "born again" is intertwined with our culture's views of personal choice and agency.

Spiritual rebirth being centered around choice becomes more about an intellectual act rather than embracing a spiritual mystery. Nevertheless, the experience of being born again is a transformative framework for many. People desiring or claiming a born again moment likely see a need to be turned away from behavior and ways of being that are harmful to themselves or others. There are others who see no need for transformation, which can also be harmful. The motivation behind the desire to be born again is about a hope for renewal. Renewal, however, is an ongoing process.

Catholic

The word "catholic" comes from the Greek word *katholikos*, meaning "universal." It was used in early Christianity to refer to the universal community of Jesus followers. Catholic with a lowercase "c" as found in the Nicene Creed and Apostles' Creed maintains this general meaning.

Uppercase "C" Catholic refers to the Roman Catholic Church. The Bishop of Rome, meaning the Pope, was gaining authority over the various Christian communities in the fifth century, as the church in Rome became more prominent. The Catholic Church became more associated with Rome, hence the Roman Catholic Church.

The Great Schism of 1054 CE resulted in a split between the Western Church and Eastern Church. The Western Church kept the "Catholic" title, and the Eastern Church became the Eastern Orthodox Church. The Protestant Reformation in the sixteenth century caused a further split between the Catholic Church and Protestants.

Charisma

Many nondenominational churches are described as charismatic in their worship style. Additionally, pastors of these churches are often said to have charisma—a word that has an interesting evolution. *Charisma* in ancient Greek means "gift of favor," and by the mid-1600s, it referred to having God-given abilities like teaching and healing. To have charisma or a charism meant to have very specific, divinely given gifts. This meaning began to fade in public usage by the 1930s, when the word more often was used to describe a person with a knack for leadership, a magnetism, or appealing personality. A few decades later, in the 1950s, it began to simply mean "charming."[24]

Building a church around a single leader, whether in a charismatic context or not, is problematic. Giving an individual sole power over a

24. Amanda Montell, *Cultish: The Language of Fanaticism* (New York: Harper Wave, 2021), 125.

community is problematic. Ancient liturgy, with room for evolution, provides a framework to allow for worship to focus on God and the gathered community, past and present, who make up the Church, the Body of Christ.

Christian

The members of the earliest Jesus communities were not considered Christians. They called themselves many things, including "the Way," "the Enslaved of God," "the body of the anointed," and "brothers and sisters." Some of this language is still being used by churches today. How these groups understood Jesus also differed. While letters and other written communication began to be shared across communities, reading overall played a small role in the communities and was always a communal activity. The early Jesus communities came together to share food, honor God, discuss their lives in a posture of compassion and support, and keep each other safe. This sounds lovely and peaceful, but it was an anti-imperial practice. To find support from small groups rather than from the Romans, whose propaganda campaigns were intended to remind those who had been conquered that the Roman Empire was their savior, was to deny the empire's authority.

The term Christian had a different meaning in the first two centuries after Jesus's death. *Christianos* is not a word that was translated but rather transliterated from Greek. To translate means to choose a word in the second language with the same or similar meaning. However, "Christian" was a new word, with no equal or similar word in other languages. Therefore, Christian is a transliteration of the original Greek, created from letter-to-letter approximations and sounds. The Greek letter chi (X) becomes "Ch" (thus the appropriate "Xmas" instead of "Christmas"). Part of "Christian" comes from the Greek root *christos*, meaning messiah in Hebrew. Messiah means "anointed with oil." In Israel, anointment with oil marked individuals' new roles in leadership as kings, prophets, or priests. The suffix "*-ian*" means "belongs to the party of." Therefore, to be a Christian means to belong to the party of the Anointed One.

For Rome, however, the emperor was the anointed one. To belong to a party that does not claim the emperor as the anointed one, or messiah, was treason. The connection is clear in the Greek. However, when *Christianos* becomes a Latin word, it becomes *christianus* and loses its connection with anointing. In Latin, to be anointed or oiled would have been *unctus*. Many years later, the Latin word *unctus* became *unction* in late Middle English, meaning to anoint or bless in a religious context. However, in those early days, the Latin word *christianus* became further removed from its original connection to messiahship and anointing. Because English Bibles were often first translated from the Latin Vulgate, we lose the original intent of what it means to be Christian: to be dangerously opposed to the oppressive political powers of the time.

The New Testament contains about one hundred and forty thousand words, depending on the translation, and *christianos* is found only three times among these tens of thousands of words. Those three instances appear (twice) in the Acts of the Apostles and once in 1 Peter. We read these texts differently when we understand that Christianity as a religion separate from Judaism did not yet exist. Instead of pointing to the Christian religion, these texts were written to members of "the party of the Anointed One."

Christianity became a formal religion in the early fourth century CE when it merged with empire through Constantine's reign. Constantine, a Roman emperor, supported Christianity. While he was baptized, there is still debate about whether he was transformed by the Christianity message or used his support for of the nascent group of believers for political gain. His support led to the legalization of Christianity and the official merger of church and political power for the first time.

Christianity began as many diverse groups of Jesus followers. These groups differed in membership, practices, and beliefs. Christianity today, two thousand years later, still includes diverse groups of Jesus followers who continue to differ in membership, practices, and beliefs.

Church

Translations in a vernacular tongue have historically created difficulties for church and state, accustomed to controlling what the general population understood about the Bible. William Tyndale, one of the first to translate the Bible into English, was tried for heresy and burned at the stake in 1536. Tyndale's translation included multiple words that authorities found problematic. For example, Tyndale translated the Greek word *ekklesia* as "congregation" rather than "church," which was seen as an attempt to undermine the Church as an authority by placing emphasis on the community rather than the hierarchy of power.

Interestingly, the Greek word *ekklesia* referred to a political assembly of citizens, meaning free male citizens. Over time, the word *ekklesia* was used in Christianity to refer to an assembly of Jesus followers and is translated into English as "church." To turn a word reserved for a gathering of free males with political decision-making power into a word for those oppressed by the Roman Empire and following in the teachings of Jesus is a powerful bit of wordplay.

The church began to call itself "catholic" in the early second century, meaning universal. Those of us who speak the Apostles' Creed during worship are accustomed to saying "I believe in . . . the holy catholic Church." Similarly, the Nicene Creed reads, "I believe in one, holy, catholic, and apostolic Church." This does not refer to Roman Catholicism but instead to this united, universal church.

Community / Association

In the days of the early Jesus followers, clubs and associations went by many names. The Greek word *koinonia* means "fellowship" or "communion"; *synodos* means "company"; *synergasia* means "cooperation" or "coworkers." The prefix *syn-* means "with," which implies the importance of gathering with each other.

Many of the "associations of the anointed" had rules and rituals, just like any other association of the time. There was an association of the anointed in Corinth, which was led by a woman named Chloe. This group is sometimes referred to as "Chloe's people" (1 Corinthians 1:11). Chloe's people, like many groups who have gathered around a common good throughout history and today, were struggling to arrange themselves. There was conflict and division among the group, so Paul wrote a letter to Chloe's people. This letter is called the First Letter to the Corinthians in the New Testament. It represents Paul's effort to give rules, rituals, and structure to Chloe's people in Corinth.

Association leaders were sometimes called mothers and fathers. The members were sometimes referred to as siblings. These associations were chosen families, and trust and love were vital. This is what Paul was saying when he told Chloe's people to love (1 Corinthians 13). The famous verse read at weddings about love being patient and kind was not originally about a union between two lovers, but was instead directed at a group of Jesus followers who were struggling to find their way as a community. Paul is telling them that love is the most important thing that will keep this group together; without love, there is nothing on which to build a community.

Creeds

Creed comes from the Latin *credo*, which means "I give my heart to." Heart here does not mean simply emotions, but instead the deepest sense of self, so a creed is an affirmation of what or to whom you give your deepest self.

Today, creeds are formal statements of faith, but the Roman Empire played a significant role in the origins of these creeds. In fact, the first seven Councils of the Church were assembled or directed by emperors. For example, in the summer of 325 CE, nearly three hundred years after the death of Jesus, bishops gathered in the Byzantine city of Nicaea, in present-day Turkey. Emperor Constantine had recently converted to Christianity, and made it the official religion of the Romans. He quickly realized there was no unified understanding of Christianity or Jesus. Constantine demanded that these men, all Christians and Roman citizens from across the empire, come to an agreement about Christian doctrine. It took a few months, but eventually this group, known as the Council of Nicaea, produced what we now call the Nicene Creed.

The Nicene Creed states Jesus is Lord, not Constantine. The fact that this creed places Jesus above emperors and all other lords is a subversive and anti-imperial statement. The fact that most Christians continue to read this out loud at every worship service is also subversive and powerful.

Throughout history, Christian creeds—many of which are still affirmed in public worship today—were created by councils of the

Church, which were in turn controlled by the government. Governments often work to maintain power and control. When government and religion begin to collude, we see systems designed to broaden that power. Without the Roman adoption of Christianity, the survival of the faith would be in question. With power comes oppression and violence, but with power also comes preservation.

◇◇◇

Cross

THE MEANING OF THE CROSS—and of Jesus's death on the cross—has been debated since the earliest communities of Jesus followers. For some Christians, the crucifixion was the most significant part of Jesus's life and ministry; other Christians focus on his teaching. Some understand Jesus as the path to a favorable afterlife, while to others, Jesus provides ethical grounding in the here and now.

Crucifixion is associated with the word "excruciating." While crucifixion predates the Roman Empire, the Romans adopted it as a punishment for criminals and rebels, crucifying hundreds of thousands of people.

During the Roman Empire, crucifixions were performed in public to warn people against challenging the power of the empire. Crucifixion was both punishment for the one who strayed from Roman order and dissuasion for any tempted to stray. Even the word "cross," or *crux*, was used as a taunt, similar to the way somebody might say "go hang yourself" today. Some Roman citizens throughout the empire had crucifixion images on their household items such as bowls or lamps as reminders to the enslaved members of the household what punishment awaited them if they disobeyed or rebelled. The image of the cross was a fear-inducing image of power.

When Jesus told his disciples to take up their cross and follow him, it was not a metaphor. Any who followed him would be violating laws of the Romans and the Temple, and at risk of crucifixion. Not surprisingly, the cross was not embraced by Jesus followers in the first century as a symbol of faith; instead, it was understood as cruel and distasteful. By the time the Gospels were being written, however, the cross had become a symbol for "the Way," referring to the early Jesus movement. The phrase "the Way" is used several times in the New Testament, particularly in the Book of Acts, before the term "Christian" became common. In Acts 9:2, Saul (later Paul) seeks permission to arrest "any who belonged to the Way," meaning early followers of Jesus. Acts 19:9 and Acts 19:23 refer to disputes and disturbances concerning the Way. Similarly, in Acts 24:14 and Acts 24:22, Paul defends himself by saying he worships "the God of our ancestors, following the Way." Followers of "the Way" metaphorically died to their old ways of life in order to live in the ways of Jesus.

Many Christians believe that Jesus had to die for the story to unfold. One argument is called substitutionary atonement, which is the belief that Jesus died in place of sinners to satisfy divine justice. This understanding has powerfully shaped Christian views of salvation, emphasizing God's justice and mercy, while also causing many Christians to feel personal shame, guilt, and moral responsibility for Jesus's suffering. Substitutionary theory, although dominant in various Christian communities, is not the only valid way to view the crucifixion. While faith in Jesus's death and resurrection can help many Christians in times of suffering and struggle, many find other ways to understand the power of Jesus being killed on the cross.

The cross has evolved in meaning. We wear crosses as symbols of belief in Jesus, his life, death, and resurrection. The earliest Christians would have seen those images as ones of government-sanctioned murder.

Pontius Pilate, who ordered the crucifixion of Jesus, was the governor of Judaea and served under Emperor Tiberius. To modern ears, crucifixion sounds barbaric and outdated. However, we still murder people to keep power structures in place today. The cross has become synonymous with Christianity, widely seen in art, in jewelry, and to symbolically denote a space as sacred to the Christian faith. Of course, the image of the cross, in many ways, has lost its anti-imperial sentiments. Instead of being an image of Roman execution and state-sanctioned brutality, it has been rebranded and commercialized into an image sold on jewelry, clothing, and home decor. The cross has been softened and profited on, often lacking its original context.

Eucharist

The word *Eucharist* comes from the Greek word *eucharistia*, meaning "thanksgiving." The word *Communion* comes from the Latin word *communio*, meaning "common" or "shared." Both of these terms are now used to refer to the sacramental act of eating bread and drinking wine following the practice instituted by Jesus during what we have come to call the Last Supper. The Last Supper took place the day before Jesus's crucifixion, and the bread and wine theologically point to his broken body and shed blood.

The Christian sacrament of Eucharist is similar to the meals shared at ancient Greco-Roman banquets, where people would gather to discuss spiritual, political, and philosophical issues of the day. Shared meals within Jesus communities during the first centuries varied, and they were often about both ritual meaning and the act of feeding. People gathered and shared meals, and varying meanings were attached to the meals. Bread and wine were not special, but instead incredibly ordinary. The use of ordinary and accessible food for the Eucharist is a theological statement about even the poor being able to participate in this meal. Additionally, some communities of Jesus followers in the early second century grew large enough that they began to have smaller meals at their morning meetings; they continued to have full meals at their evening meetings. The sacrament of Eucharist became more standardized over time, and bread and wine continue to be the most common elements used.

The early church understood those participating in the Eucharist as re-membering—gathering again—as the body of Christ. A sacrament in ancient times was an oath of allegiance to the emperor by a soldier, which was made visible by branding the soldier's arm or forehead, and the Latin Vulgate translated the Greek word for "mystery" as *sacramentum*. This linguistic connection between mystery and sacrament point to our participation in the sacrament of Eucharist as a means of connecting to the mystery of God.

The Romans had a practice of libation similar to our sacrament of Eucharist. In this libation, a liquid—milk, honey, or wine—was poured onto the ground or over a sacred object before events. The Roman libation was seen as demonstration of political allegiance to the emperor, similar to reciting a pledge of allegiance or singing a national anthem before an event. This Roman libation was also seen as a religious act to call upon the favor of the gods on behalf of the emperor. To refuse to participate in this ritual of libation was an act of treason.

For Jesus communities to turn this ritual of libation into their own ritual of commemoration of their own Lord was a bold statement about their allegiance to Jesus, not Rome. When we drink wine and bread in worship today, we are engaging in the long tradition of remembering all those who have suffered and are suffering at the hands of those with power. The Eucharist, eating the body in the form of bread and drinking the blood in the form of wine, calls us into awareness of this oppression and suffering, past and present. Eucharist is both a partaking and a call to action. Eucharist is about sharing a meal with a community that believes the world can be different from the status quo.

Evangelicalism

The term evangelical comes from the Greek word *euangelion*, meaning "good news" or "gospel." *Eu* means "good," and *angelion* means "message." The word entered Latin as *evangelium*, came into Old French as *evangile*, and eventually formed the English word *evangelical* in the late Middle Ages. Throughout this time, it remained affiliated with "gospel." During the Reformation, evangelical came to be used as a description for reformers' emphasis on the authority of scripture and the Gospels. In many German-speaking areas today, *evangelisch* continues to be the word used for "Protestant." I am a Lutheran in the United States; the official name of my branch of Lutheranism is the Evangelical Lutheran Church in America (ELCA), reflecting the denomination's German and Protestant roots. However, there has been some conversation and debate within the ELCA about removing the "Evangelical" from our name because of the connotations it has taken on in America.

The recent phenomenon called "evangelicalism" is a movement more than a formal institution. In the eighteenth and nineteenth centuries in the United States, evangelical identity evolved to highlight personal "born again" experiences, ultimate biblical authority, and evangelism. Evangelism simply means to spread the good news; however, the evangelical movement expanded beyond simple evangelism. In the United States, evangelicalism has become as much a political movement as a religious one, contributing to the rise of the Religious

Right in the 1970s and 1980s. Politically, evangelical values include things like opposition to abortion and promotion of "traditional" family values.

Evangelicalism has a long history that is intertwined with the history of fundamentalism. Both began as fringe movements in the 1900s, rising to prominence with the Moral Majority in the 1980s. Billy Graham, an evangelical who broadcast his preaching on radio and television from the mid-1980s to early 2000s, contributed to the rise of evangelicalism. During the mid-1980s, as the tension between fundamentalism and science grew, United States coins began to be impressed with "In God We Trust" and the Pledge of Allegiance began to include the line "one nation under God." The United States' identity was being influenced by culture's ongoing tension between conservative Christianity and science.

This debate became more polarized in the second half of the twentieth century with the civil rights movements, feminism, and Roe v. Wade. Throughout those years, fundamentalists and evangelicals began to gain political power in the United States. They began by gaining seats on school boards, and then seats in state legislatures and Congress. There was a rise in evangelical chaplains in the military and on college and university campuses. Evangelical Christians have influenced the outcome of recent presidential elections, most notably those of Ronald Reagan, George W. Bush, and Donald Trump.

The number of evangelical Christians has been in decline since the mid-2000s,[25] but this is part of a broader decrease in people who identify as Christian in general. A 2018 poll estimated that one in three people

25. Pew Research Center. "Decline of Christianity in the U.S. Has Slowed, May Have Leveled Off." *Pew Research Center: Religion & Public Life*, February 26, 2025. https://www.pewresearch.org/religion/2025/02/26/decline-of-christianity-in-the-us-has-slowed-may-have-leveled-off/.

who were raised in American evangelical households leave the tradition as adults.[26] The movement of adults who left the evangelical beliefs of their childhood behind is called "exvangelicalism."[27] Still, evangelicalism remains a political force that cannot be ignored.

Faith

THE GREEK WORD *pistis* is best translated as "trust" or "loyalty." However, many biblical translators have instead chosen to translate it as "faith" or "belief." *Belief* comes from the Old English *be loef*, from which we get *belove*. Before the 1600s, to believe was a synonym to belove, meaning "to hold dear." To belove God is very different from believing in God.

Faith is similar to belief. Faith is related to the Latin words *fidelitas* and *fiducia*, the root of our English word *fidelity*. *Fidelity* is often used in the context of marriage and is about remaining faithful. In other words, faithfulness is about loyalty. To have faith does not mean believing a specific set of truths as outlined by a book or group, but instead speaks to commitment and loyalty to God.

Loyalty requires trust, so the opposite of faithfulness can be seen as mistrust, which is another way to say anxiety. When we lose trust in a parent, partner, child, or friend, we are anxious. When we are in a state of mistrust about anything, we are in a state of anxiety. Jesus makes a

26. Daniel Cox, "Are White Evangelicals Sacrificing the Future in Search of the Past?," *FiveThirtyEight*, January 24, 2018, https://fivethirtyeight.com/features/are-white-evangelicals-sacrificing-the-future-in-search-of-the-past/.
27. Sarah McCammon, *The Exvangelicals: Loving, Living, and Leaving the White Evangelical Church* (New York: St. Martin's Press, 2024).

connection between faithfulness and anxiety when he says, "you of little faith . . . do not worry" (Matthew 6:30–31, Luke 12:28–29). Having faith is about loyalty and trust, the antidotes to anxiety and worry.

Family Values

Conservative Christianity often uses the phrase "family values," lifting the Bible as evidence of this familial ethic. However, the Bible does not provide evidence of a nuclear family in the ways it is commonly understood. If the Adam and Eve story is taken literally, then their children had to have had sex with each other. Abraham impregnated his slave, who was not his wife. David had multiple wives; Solomon had hundreds of concubines; and Mary was an unwed, pregnant teenager. Jesus likely was unwed and without children. The Gospel of Matthew tells of Jesus rejecting his family. Paul often aligned himself against marriage. The Bible has a complicated view of "family," to say the least.

Families within the Roman Empire were set up similarly to the larger society, with a male head-of-household. This concept was called the *paterfamilias*. The emperor was the *paterfamilias* of Roman territories and the male head-of-household was the *paterfamilias* of his household, including his wife, children, and enslaved. The *paterfamilias* had authority over every aspect of their household's life: financial, social, legal, and disciplinary.

When some Christians today refer to family values, they are often pointing back to the values modeled in the *paterfamilias* system enforced by the Roman Empire. This patriarchal model is not the entirety of the *paterfamilias* reality. We must be careful when we romanticize this social and familial arrangement, as it is dangerous to many members of the family. The typical family also included enslaved members of the household. About one hundred thousand Judeans are said to have been enslaved by Romans after the fall of Jerusalem at the hands of the Roman military in 70 CE. Enslavement awaited those vulnerable to debt or inability to pay taxes; this would have comprised a large portion of the population, including Jesus of Nazareth, a lowly day laborer at risk of being unable to survive on his wages alone.

The promotion of traditional family values often ignores the problematic, abusive aspects of the male-dominated system. The system that incorporated the exploitation and abuse of the enslaved in the Roman Empire found its way into biblical texts, and these Christian texts were foundational in the justification of enslavement two thousand years later in the transatlantic slave trade. To ignore the roles the Bible and Christianity have had in the inhumane history of enslavement would be cruel and unjust. A Christian faith that incorporates these types of family values can be inhumane, unethical, and dangerous.

Family values are often a way to reinforce gender roles. While some women, by choice or necessity, quit paid jobs to stay at home and raise their children, each family should have the freedom to choose the pattern appropriate for them. The American legal system does not acknowledge domestic labor, historically viewed as women's labor, as valuable compared to the paid employment historically reserved for men. Staying home to care for the home and/or children is a noble choice and nonstop labor, yet our legal system does not see this as an equal contribution to family life or the economy. A male head-of-household often benefits from the unseen and unpaid labor of the members of his household.

Family and economy continue to be linked in every way. Corporate leaders may refer to their employees as "family" in a manipulative effort to make the organization appear close-knit. Make no mistake: patriarchy and capitalism cannot survive without one another. Patriarchy and capitalism oppress anyone who is not a male with economic power. Feminists acknowledge the fact that our patriarchal-capitalist system also hurts males, even those with economic power.

A Christianity that doesn't speak truth to power is a Christianity that encourages its communities to keep the cycle of domination in motion. We must acknowledge that family values rooted in a system with a male head-of-household, in its ancient and current forms, can be deeply abusive to other members of the household or family. To hold up traditional family values is to ignore this history. People who disobeyed the Roman Empire's paterfamilias system were crucified, including the one Christians claim as the Messiah, Jesus of Nazareth.

Fundamentalism

Christian fundamentalism is a theological movement that claims to uphold foundational Christian doctrines through a literal interpretation of the Bible. Historically, it can be understood best as a reaction to modernity—an age of philosophy, beginning in the Enlightenment era, that questioned assumption of authority in favor of scientific proof and reason. Scientific inquiry and modernity quickly aligned against the teachings of the Church and against its style of language. Poetic literacy began to decline. The symbolism, metaphor, and analogy of ancient sacred texts began to be ignored in favor of more literal and scientific interpretations. Language became a way to communicate accuracy and facts. Language became linear, direct, and simple.

Fundamentalism was born from this shift in language. As a direct byproduct of the Enlightenment, fundamentalists became the first

Christians to read the Bible as a factual and literal text rather than a truthful and sacred text. Despite Christian fundamentalism's rejection of much of science, most notably favoring creationism over evolution, fundamentalism's readings of the Bible come from the rise of scientific reasoning—reading for literal, provable truths. This approach stands in opposition with the ways ancient people understood biblical stories as testimonies to greater truth, not literal fact. The story of these truths was sometimes historical and other times symbolic in nature, pointing to understandings about power structures, oppression, and humanity's relationship to divinity. Bible scholar Pete Enns writes, "What if God is actually fine with the Bible just as it is . . . the messy, troubling, weird, and ancient Bible that we actually have? Maybe this Bible has something to show us about our own sacred journey of faith."[28]

Bishop James Ussher, Church of Ireland Archbishop in the 1600s, calculated the age of the universe by totaling the ages of patriarchs in the Bible, concluding that creation began in 3963 BCE. Fundamentalism did not begin with Ussher, but his effort to apply scientific thought to the Bible is a direct influence of modernity's focus on rationality. Fundamentalism took off in the 1800s, and has gained power since. As the Enlightenment era and subsequent periods challenged Christianity's authority over knowledge, fundamentalism attempted to reclaim and keep the power of its authority. The movement was—and is—an attempt to keep Christianity as the dominant worldview. Paradoxically, Christian fundamentalists used scientific ways of thinking to argue against scientific ways of thinking.

Christian fundamentalism in the United States began as fringe movements around 1900. Over the decades, fundamentalist groups became more socially and politically conservative for a variety of rea-

28. Peter Enns, *The Bible Tells Me So: Why Defending Scripture Has Made Us Unable to Read It* (New York: HarperOne, 2015), 9.

sons, with keen fixation on such topics as abortion. In the same way, fundamentalists became single-mindedly focused on the inerrancy of scripture, equating truth with fact and myth with untruth. Of course, myth is not the opposite of truth, but a way of speaking truth non-literally. Nevertheless, fundamentalists do not embrace myth as meaningful, insistent upon absolute and narrow truth. They seek to hold the Bible to the same standards as modern science, but the Bible was never meant to operate this way. Both secular modernists and the Christian fundamentalists view the Bible without nuance missing the truths conveyed within these ancient myths. Rethinking, questioning, or embracing biblical complexity risks crumbling fundamentalist beliefs. The foundation of fundamentalism—an infallible Bible—is easily proven to be fragile.

The language of fundamentalism found its way into public and political discourse, through multi-generational efforts to build institutions of power beginning with the use of radio in the 1930s. Consequently, religious rhetoric has become political rhetoric: phrases like "family values" belong to both religious fundamentalists and political parties. The Republican Party and fundamentalist Christianity have long collaborated.[29] Fundamentalists gained political power, working to undo much of the political work of modernity, particularly policies that support women, encourage racial justice, and acknowledge scientific discoveries. Christian fundamentalists, who share a history of early Christians gathered in opposition to oppression and power, have become the powerful oppressors.

◇◇◇

29. April Ajoy, *Star-Spangled Jesus: Leaving Christian Nationalism and Finding a True Faith* (Nashville: Worthy Publishing, 2024), 33, 36, 55, 57.

Grace

Grace is a word that gets thrown around a lot in Christianity. The English word grace comes from the Latin *gratia*, meaning "favor" or "goodwill." In Old French, *grace* meant favor, mercy, or elegance. It passed into Middle English to mean favor from a superior, beauty, or virtue. In Christian theology, grace has come to mean God's unearned favor toward humanity. The word often translated as "grace" in the New Testament is the Greek word *charis*, which is related to the word *chara* meaning "joy" and *charizomai* meaning "to give freely."

We hear a lot about grace from Paul, most notably in Ephesians 2:8 when he tells his readers that they are saved by grace. The early church father Augustine connected grace as necessary for salvation because of original sin. Of course, there were opponents to this theological stance. For example, Pelagius argued that humans were capable of choosing righteously without God's grace. The Church taught that grace came through the sacraments like baptism and the Eucharist.

During the Protestant Reformation, reformers like Martin Luther and John Calvin reclaimed grace as something unearned, and *sola gratia*, meaning "grace alone," became a Protestant doctrine. The idea that human deeds or rituals earned God's favor, or grace, was rejected by reformers. This was a radical idea for medieval Christians who were told that good works earned God's love and eternal salvation.

Linguistically, the use of the word grace continues to be about unearned forgiveness and mercy. For example, a grace period is given freely in financial and legal contexts. Similarly, we say grace, or give thanks, before receiving the gift of a meal. Acknowledging God's grace allows us to understand salvation as something we receive, not something human beings control.

Heresy

The Greek word *hairesis* means "choice," as in choosing a different school of thought. Originally, the word did not carry a negative connotation and was often used to refer to Greek philosophical schools and systems of thought. It would be translated as party or school as we might today refer to a political party or school of thought. It was transliterated into Latin as *haereses* and eventually into Old French as *heresie*. Ultimately, it became our English word *heresy*.

When *heresy* was translated into Latin and Christian writers began to use it, the word took on the negative connotation of having an opinion different from official church doctrine. This understanding of heresy originates in the context of religion. The idea that heresy resulted in exclusion from the group was not present until Tertullian, a teacher in a Jesus community from Carthage in the Roman province of Africa. Tertullian wrote around the late second century that a heretic was no longer considered part of the group. Until this point, the division of thought was not grounds for expulsion.

However, the title heretic was not always used to refer to someone who was pushed to the outside of the group and a criminal, so we cannot read all biblical texts with this negative connotation over it. For example, some versions of 1 Corinthians 11:18 translate *hairesis* as "divisions," including the NRSV: "I hear that there are divisions among you." Paul is expressing that there seems to be a possibility of the Corinthian community dividing into schools of different thought.

Later, a charge of heresy was a legal charge, often punishable by death. Reformers were deemed heretics aligned against official Church doctrine. Early translators of the Bible, like William Tyndale, were considered heretical for putting the biblical texts into languages common people could read. Witchcraft has been deemed heretical by the Church. The list of heretics and heresies is long. Who has been considered a heretic has always been culturally and politically situated. Heresy is what exists outside dominant beliefs or doctrine in any given moment or place. Thankfully, in most parts of the world today, heretics are no longer sentenced to death.

◊◊◊

Holy

The word *holy* has become so common and familiar that we have forgotten some of its significance. *Holy* comes from the Anglo-Saxon root *hal*—as in "hallowed be thy name" in the Lord's Prayer—which has associations with "whole," "healthy," and "holistic." Given that the word *religion*, meaning to re-align or make whole, is connected to being whole, it's no surprise that *holy* is similar in meaning.

If we know our etymology, we know that the word *holidays* is an abbreviation of "holy days." "Happy Holy Days"—or "Happy Holidays"—could be considered as a more Christian greeting because Christmas is not the only holiday being celebrated in the church; it is a season of many holy days, including the twelve days of Christmas that begin on Christmas Day and end on January 5, the eve of the Epiphany. Many churches celebrate other holy days in this season, including the Feast of Saint Stephen, the Feast of Saint John, and the Feast of the Holy Innocents. Saying "Happy Holidays" includes all Christian holidays in this season and allows for respect for other religions. Even saying "hello" is linguistically connected to holy, so to say "hello" is to wish someone health and wholeness.[30]

The words for heal and whole come from the same word as holy, suggesting that these are all related to living a whole life. Interestingly, *salvation* relates to the Latin *salvare* meaning "to save," and *salvere* meaning "to heal." (This is where we get the word *salve*.) In the second century, salvation had nothing to do with the afterlife but with being saved from—healed from—earthly suffering, which was too often a consequence of violent and oppressive Roman occupation. Knowing how early Jesus followers understood salvation, and understanding the connection among the words salvation, holy, and wholeness, we can appreciate "holy living" as ways that bring wholeness to our earthly life.

People have a need for community, ritual, embodiment, emotional expression, and mystery. To live religiously or to seek holiness is simply to live intentionally with this sense of wholeness. Religion and holiness come in many forms and belong to us all.

Jesus's Long Hair

Art, like language, is a method of communication and meaning-making. Jesus is one of the most commonly painted figures in Western art. In the church I attend, as in many European and American churches, images of Jesus are everywhere—and nearly every image is a white man with long hair, an inaccurate image. First and foremost, Jesus was a Jewish man raised in what is now the northern part of

30. Gary Eberle, *Dangerous Words: Talking about God in an Age of Fundamentalism* (Boston, MA: Trumpeter, 2007), 115.

Israel. He did not have porcelain white skin with blue eyes, as we often see him portrayed.

We also often see Jesus with long hair, an unlikely trait. About four hundred years ago, third century paintings of Jesus were discovered in the catacombs of St. Domitian in Rome. These paintings depict Jesus as short-haired and beardless. In the last decade, another early painting of Jesus was discovered on a ruined church in Israel, dated in the sixth century. This image depicts Jesus with shorter, curly hair. We begin to see Jesus depicted with long hair and a beard in the fourth century, influenced by depictions of Greek and Roman Gods, especially Zeus.

Christianity merged with power, and power influenced how we depict Jesus in our art. White, blue-eyed, bearded, and long-haired Jesus is far from what Jesus would have looked like. We all want God to look like us, and the dominant "us" is largely formed by power structures. As for me and my house, we avoid buying Christmas decorations, nativity sets, and crucifixes with white bodies. These images take me further away from who Jesus was, a Middle Eastern man of little means who was murdered by those in power.

Lector

During the early days of the Jesus communities, many enslaved people were forced into literacy labor, often serving as scribes, copyists, and readers to meet their enslavers' needs and desires. Today, we think of literacy as an erudite value, but writing was an act of physical labor in the first centuries when Jesus stories were being written down. Scribes and copyists typically sat crisscross with the tablet on their knee; they would hunch over to write on the tablet many hours a day. Lighting was not always ideal. This was physically difficult work.

Consequently, enslaved and formerly enslaved individuals in early Jesus communities often filled literacy roles. Reading aloud the biblical texts, or the early letters and Jesus testimonies written on codex, was a performance of sorts. A person in a literary role would have been well-versed in the texts they read at gatherings of Jesus communities, using inflection, hand gestures, and body language as the community listened to and watched. Early readers also used props, including members of the audience and furniture, to tell the stories. In those communities, when many members had poor eyesight or could not read, the labor of readers was vital to the faith of Jesus followers.

Eventually, readers came to be called lectors. Revelation 1:3 even opens with a statement naming those who read aloud as blessed, a reference to readers (lectors) in the community. In this way, low-status and enslaved people contributed to the spread and interpretation of the New Testament long before it was written down.

◇◇◇

Liturgy

The earliest Jesus followers debated more about right rituals than about right beliefs. In fact, in the first and second centuries, Jesus communities found orthopraxy, the correct conduct of liturgy, more important than orthodoxy, correct belief and doctrine. Of course, becoming too focused on orthopraxis can, and has, led some Christian sects to believe that we can earn our worth through good deeds and right actions. Today, this is reinforced by the values of modern capitalism, which keep people earning their income, wellbeing, and self-worth through work.

Rituals at their core are deeply human. Rituals make up a liturgical life. Liturgy teaches us that this repetition is holy if we give it intention and attention. What is mundane is also sacred. Sacred means to "set aside" or to "make holy." The item or activity is not in itself sacred, but is made that way by associating it with the divine. Washing dishes, mowing the lawn, or taking the bus can be set aside and made holy if we are intentional about it. And when these rituals are made sacred, they become the liturgies of our lives.

Sacred liturgies are small acts in a specific and intentional order that make up public worship and church life. The word *liturgy* comes from the Greek word *leitourgia*, which is a combination of the words *leitos*, meaning "public," and *ergon*, meaning "work" or "deed." *Liturgy* literally means "public work" or "work on behalf of the people." In ancient Greece, this public work was seen in the form of public service and civic engagement. In Christianity, liturgy has evolved to refer to the communal worship pattern and calendar of the church. Liturgy refers to the order of a given service of worship, and is also about the seasons, celebrations, and observances of the church year. Liturgy emphasizes the work of those gathered, meaning it has a lot to do with community. A liturgy is how a community organizes itself for prayer.

Some reject the notion of religion, church, ritual, and liturgy. They can't comprehend this way of gathering in modern times. However, many people eat the same oatmeal at the same time each morning. They exercise a certain number of hours each week. They put on a jersey and show up to cheer on their favorite team each week. Every spring they clean out their garage and plant a new garden. They have daily, weekly, monthly, and annual habits that make up their lives. They do these things "religiously." They are committed to these habits, and their life feels fuller because of these rituals. This is a ritually ordered life.

Liturgy is the way in which we order our gatherings. It can be ornate and full of symbolic actions, or it can be simple and quiet in its movements and flow. As one who attends a liturgical church, I find liturgy a steady and slow burn toward a deep and steady faith. Knowing the flow of the liturgy from week to week allows me to meditate on experiences and words within the service.

Liturgy, if done well, tells a story. There is a rhythm to liturgy. The liturgical calendar flows in an annual cycle reflecting the Christian story. The liturgical year begins with Advent in the four to seven weeks leading up to Christmas Eve. The Christmas season, which lasts from December 25 to January 6, is followed by Epiphany from January 6 to the beginning of Lent. Epiphany and Lent are separated by Shrove Tuesday and Ash Wednesday; Lent is the forty days (not counting Sundays) leading up to Holy Week, and Holy Week is the week before Easter Day. Holy Week and Easter, of course, observe the last week of Jesus's life, Jesus's death, and Jesus's resurrection. Easter is a season of fifty days and followed by Pentecost, which celebrates the indwelling of the Holy Spirit and the beginning of the spread of the Gospel. Following Pentecost is Ordinary Time, which focuses on the mission of the church. Each of these seasons—Advent, Christmas, Epiphany, Lent, Holy Week, Easter, Pentecost, and Ordinary Time—has a symbolic liturgical color used in church and a cycle of scripture readings to coincide with the season.

This liturgy—the flow of prayers, scripture, reflection, singing, and receiving communion—is built by a community of people over time, hence the ancient context of liturgy being the work of the public. Liturgy gives a space for the community's worship of God. The church's long history of liturgy, with room for evolution, provides a framework for the people, past, present, and future, who have gathered to worship as the Body of Christ. For example, Christians have sung the *Kyrie* for centuries: "Lord, have mercy; Christ, have mercy; Lord, have mercy." When we sing this ancient text each week, we join the choir of those who sang before us and those who will sing after us. Liturgy remains when we do not. Living a liturgical life transcends time and connects us to those outside of our own lifetime. We are entering into a pattern that people of the past, present, and future have been, are, and will be a part of.

◊◇◊

Love

When a concept is culturally important to a group of people, it is reflected in the language. For example, snow is a critical part of life in Arctic regions. The Sámi languages, belonging to the Indigenous people of Scandinavia, contain almost two hundred words related to snow and ice. Inuit dialects use the word *aput* to describe snow on the ground, *piqsirpoq* for drifting snow, and *qimuqsuq* is snowdrift. Similarly, camels are important in desert life, and Arabic uses over one hundred sixty different words for camel depending on the camel's age, sex, color, and purpose—including *jamal* for a generic camel, *naqah* for a female camel, *hajīn* for a racing camel, and *ghadā* for a camel that walks smoothly. The Chinese have many terms for tea. Hawaiian has a variety of words and compound words to describe different types and spiritual meanings of water.

In English, we stretch the word "love." I can say I love my daughters and I love my morning coffee. The same word is used, but I obviously do not mean the same thing in both contexts. In ancient Greek, the language of the New Testament, there are many words for "love." *Eros* is a romantic and sexual love. *Storge* is familial love. *Philia* is a friendship kind of love. *Agape* is unconditional or divine love.

The word *love* has a complicated story in the Bible. There are many Greek, Hebrew, and Aramaic words that have been translated into English as "love." As we know, love is multivalent, and the complexities of biblical translations for love extend beyond the various translations. For example, the word for love in Deuteronomy's repetitions of the injunction to "love your God" was used in the ancient Near East in a political context to describe loyalty to the political party of the day. Once again, we see political lingo being transferred to religious and spiritual contexts.

An interesting example of how we lose meaning in translation can be found in John 21:15–17. Jesus asks Simon Peter three times, "Do you love me?" Each time, Simon Peter replies, "Yes." At face value, Jesus appears desperate for Simon Peter's love. What we miss in our English translations is that the first two times Jesus asks, "Do you *agape* me?," meaning "Do you love me unconditionally?" Both times, Simon Peter responds to Jesus by saying, "I *philia* you," meaning, "I love you as a friend." The third time Jesus asks him if he loves him, he meets Simon Peter where he is at and asks, "Do you *philia* me?" Peter felt hurt by Jesus's shift in language choice, likely because he knows he cannot admit to the unconditional love Jesus is asking for. Peter says, "You know everything; you know that I philia you." In other words, Peter is being honest with Jesus by telling him he cares for him deeply in the context of a friendship, but he cannot express the unconditional, divine kind of love Jesus asks. Read with the Greek in mind, this scene tells us something very different from its superficial, presumed meaning.

Translation issues surrounding the word *love* extend beyond the Bible and Jesus's lifetime, too. William Tyndale (1494–1536) is best known for translating the Bible into English. He was the first person to translate significant parts of the Bible into English directly from the original Hebrew and Greek texts, rather than the Latin Vulgate. His work was foundational for later English translations of the Bible. Tyndale believed that all persons should have access to the Bible into their own language, but his work was deemed heretical by the Catholic Church and King Henry VIII because it challenged the Church's authority. Putting the Bible in the hands of common people lessened the Church's authority, but Tyndale also made specific translation choices that were not popular with the Church.

Tyndale translated the Greek word *agape* as "love" rather than "charity," emphasizing an inner emotion rather than an outward action. At the time, the Church focused on works (charity to the poor, indulgences, prayers, etc.) as a means of salvation. Tyndale's choice not to translate *agape* as "charity" supported Martin Luther's stance against this doctrine, and Tyndale's translation that seemingly neglected the action of charity further angered those in power.

Martyr

Martyr is from the Greek word for witness. In Greek, martyr can refer to one who testifies or witnesses something, which is why this meaning is sometimes found in English using words like witness or testimony. However, in some places, as in the Book of Revelation, a martyr is one who dies on behalf of their witness or testimony—Jesus (Revelation 1:5), Antipas (Revelation 2:13), and the souls of those slaughtered (Revelation 6:9).

The early Jesus communities circulated many stories of martyrdom; their preoccupation with stories of martyrs would lead one to believe they were being killed by the scores, but the Roman Empire was not overly interested in killing members of early Jesus communities in the first two centuries. Still, these early followers of Jesus were preoccupied with stories of dying for their cause like Jesus.

Members of Jesus communities—not yet called Christians—were executed, but this was not common practice. In fact, Pliny, a first century governor of a Roman territory, wrote to Emperor Trajan asking what he should do with the *christianus*, the Latin phrase referring to the resistant groups from Judea. These letters make clear that Pliny gave people many opportunities to claim loyalty to the empire before imprisoning or executing them, showing that the empire was not actively seeking out members of these groups. Trajan specifically responds that these people should not be hunted, but only punished if they are brought before Pliny and do not show repentance.

To suffer and be killed because of membership in a Jesus community made one a martyr, and this identity was a clear statement that you were truly *christianus*. Remember that this term was not yet a label for a unified religion but instead a political term used by those in power to name these emerging groups proclaiming another messiah besides the emperor. To boldly claim you are *christianus* was another way to say you were not Roman.

Gladiator fights in the first two centuries commonly forced the enslaved to participate in this dangerous spectacle. Eventually, men would volunteer for these gladiator combat events to prove how Roman they were—in other words, to show how courageous and strong they were. To win a gladiator match was a way to prove your honor and virtue in a society that provided little opportunity to prove your worth otherwise. The gladiator belonged to Rome, and those who lost were martyrs for Rome's cause. Dying for Rome in these fights became a symbol of Roman loyalty just as much as winning did.

In a similar way, members of Jesus communities claimed their own martyrs to oppose the Roman gladiator martyrs. Like gladiators, they voluntarily died for their cause. These martyr stories in the face of suffering in the empire allowed Jesus communities to have a sense of control over their suffering and oppression. The idea of dying willingly created a courageous and virtuous martyr rather than a victim, and was an anti-imperial stance.

Myth

We often equate truth and fact, but linguistically these two words have had separate histories. What is true is not always factual. A simple example to demonstrate this difference can be found in Aesop's fable of the tortoise and the hare. The slow tortoise races the quick hare, ultimately winning the race. This story is not factual, meaning the story is not based on an actual tortoise racing an actual hare at some point in history. Instead, this story reveals the truth that slow and steady wins the race. This story is true without being factual.

Myth comes from the Greek word *mythos* and Latin word *mythus*, meaning "story," and didn't appear in the English language until the 1800s—during a time shaped by the Age of Enlightenment. Curiously, it came into the English language at a time when literal truth was of great significance, and it served to mean something that is not literally true. Truth and myth were pitted against each other, and myth was seen as more frivolous and unnecessary.

Science may be the language of facts, but myth is the language of truth. German theologian Ethelbert Stauffer put it this way: "[Myth] speaks of heavenly things in an earthly way, and of earthly things in a heavenly way."[31] Myth, therefore, is every bit as complex and necessary as science as a tool to gain and construct knowledge. Knowledge comes in the form of thoughts, but it also comes from emotion, experience, and embodiment. This is the part of human truth that myth speaks to and about. Myth uses narrative and poetry to convey meaning, as opposed to logic and mathematics. If science is a way to know and communicate

31. Ethelbert Stauffer, *Christ and the Caesars: Historical Sketches* (Eugene, OR: Wipf & Stock, 1952), 16.

that which is rational, myth is a way to know and communicate wisdom. Myth provides wisdom about deeply human things—birth, coming of age, marrying, arranging communal life, forgiveness, grief, death.

The "Tortoise and the Hare" is a myth that contains truth. We could simply say that "slow and steady wins the race," but this feels abstract to the human mind. Myths were made for humans, or perhaps humans were made for myth. The mythologist Joseph Campbell speaks on the connection between myth and metaphor: "God is a metaphor for mystery that absolutely transcends all human categories of thought. Even the categories of being and nonbeing."[32] There is something about human existence that inherently connects us with myth, and myth is the language that gets us close to communicating about God. "The Tortoise and the Hare" myth has the power to last centuries—and, in fact, has. Christianity, too, contains myth, which has the potential to be eternal.

Humans have found many ways to bring myths into the material world, and in religious settings we often see this in rituals and sacred objects. For example, the Bible includes myths around bathing as a means of moral cleansing, which we have come to know as one of the meanings of baptism. This practice of bathing and a font with water hold little importance until they are connected to myth. Myth also connects us to each other. Baptism communicates the truth about identity and group belonging. Myths are meaning-making tools, and humans are meaning-making machines. Myth, which is sometimes factual but always true, is the language of religion. English professor and author Gary Eberle says, "Myth provides the narrative thread that guides us through the labyrinth of our lives."[33] To say that the

32. Phil Cousineau, ed., *The Hero's Journey: Joseph Campbell on his Life and Work* (Novato, CA), 161.
33. Gary Eberle, *Dangerous Words: Talking about God in an Age of Fundamentalism* (Boston, MA: Trumpeter, 2007), 100.

Bible is mythical is not an insult. To take the Bible seriously means taking myth seriously.

Orthodox

The word orthodox comes to us from the Greek language. *Orthos* means "straight" or "correct," and *doxa* means "opinion" or "belief." Literally, orthodox means "correct opinion or belief." It was mostly used in Greek philosophical contexts where "correct opinions" were debated and discussed, and entered Christian discourse as theological disagreements emerged in the Church. *Orthodox* was a term used in contrast to heresy. People who considered themselves to have the right beliefs labeled themselves as orthodox and labeled those who disagreed with them as heretical.

We can already see how this is problematic and steeped in power structures. Who gets to decided what "correct belief" is? This is especially dangerous considering people deemed heretics have been sentenced to death at certain points in history.

The term *orthodox* became a formal title after the Great Schism of 1054 CE. The Eastern Orthodox Church split from the Roman Catholic Church over theological and liturgical differences. The Eastern Orthodox Church believed themselves to have the correct beliefs and right worship. The Eastern Orthodox Church emphasized theological concepts like mystery and the Trinity, and they rejected the notion of a single leader like the Pope. They considered both scripture and tradition as authoritative and worshipped in a highly liturgical style. The Eastern Orthodox Church includes branches like Greek Orthodox, Russian Orthodox, among others.

Protestant

The Protestant Reformation began in 1517 when Martin Luther, a university professor and monk, is said to have nailed his Ninety-five Theses on the door of the Castle Church in Wittenberg, Germany. The theses were Luther's effort to reform the church from his place within the Roman Catholic establishment. Luther had no intention of beginning a new religious entity; nevertheless, Luther was considered a heretic by Pope Leo X and excommunicated. Holy Roman Emperor Charles V declared Luther a heretic and an outlaw, banned his writings, and made it a crime for anyone to assist him. Yet When Luther was asked to renounce his writings, he famously refused, saying, "Here I stand, I can do no other."

As is often the case with banned writings, banning Luther's ideas did not stop them from spreading, and Protestantism was born. Protestant clearly has "protest" as its root. While it may not always be immediately visible, a significant part of the Protestant identity—and Christian identity in general—is its foundation of protesting oppressive systems and critiquing those in positions of power. Protestant ideals, like individual conscience, have shaped political aspirations of democracy and have served as a backbone of many Western political systems. Ethics like those rooted in Calvinism have influenced political discourse by emphasizing personal responsibility and morality. Protestant Christians have been central voices in discourse and activism surrounding abolition, civil rights, reproductive rights, and immigration.

With Protestantism's political influence has come political power, including its alignment with and perpetuation of oppressive systems. Many sociologists connect the beginnings of modern capitalist values with the Protestant Reformation's connection between godly blessings to earthly blessings. In other words, the Protestant Reformation was the beginning of viewing monetary gains as evidence of God's good graces; wealth and profit were considered evidence of hard work and God's blessings, therefore those without money were assumed to not be working hard or blessed by God. Additionally, this ethic can be traced to the theological development of the prosperity gospel as well as the cultural projection of elitism. Of course, hard work is neither a straight line to economic prosperity nor to spiritual well-being.

The Protestant work ethic's emphasis on ambition and competition—and its role in the rise of capitalism—were fundamental to the publishing of the first self-help book, *Self-Help,* in 1859. The book's first line read: "Heaven helps those who help themselves."[34] Protestantism also fed the concept of the American Dream (the individual pursuit of achievement) and of Manifest Destiny (the U.S. expansion of white culture and colonization across the lands that now form the United States). Today, Protestantism has a wide variety of expressions, theologies, and cultural norms. Thousands of distinct Protestant denominations and groups exist globally. In the U.S., mainline Protestant denominations continue to have social and political influence.

◇◇◇

Redemption

Many Christian communities use the words *repent* and *redeem* in conjunction with *sin.* The understanding in these communities is that repentance, or admitting our wrongdoing and feeling remorse—must follow sin so that then we can be redeemed—meaning forgiven and saved from

34. Amanda Montell, *Cultish: The Language of Fanaticism* (New York: Harper Wave, 2021), 175.

sin. Of course, this is the subject of theological debate: If an unconditionally loving God does not need our confession or remorse to extend forgiveness, then what consequence will compel us not to sin in the future? If God does not need our repentance, how will we be transformed to live with changed behavior?

To understand the word *redemption*, we must know that enslavement was part of the social fabric of the Hebrew Bible. A male relative could buy an individual out of enslavement, and this relative was considered a *go'el*, or redeemer. Additionally, redemption was the term used when an enslaver bought back an enslaved person who they had previously sold to another enslaver—for example, when an enslaved person was deemed to have misbehaved (according to their enslaver).

In the Hebrew Bible, redemption is about God buying back a person or community that has been enslaved, including those times when God has given over the people to be enslaved by another power (such as the Assyrian or Babylonian Empire). Isaiah 48:20 says that God redeems his servant, Jacob (Israel). Viewed in context, the word *servant* implies enslavement, from which God "buys back" Israel. The New Testament writers extend this meaning of redemption, often referring to believers as enslaved to God (see Romans 6:22, for example). To redeem means to set free from literal enslavement, but it also more generally means to be set free from any kind of bondage or captivity. During Jesus's time, the ancient Israelites were captives of the Roman occupation.

Christian theology is diverse, and we continue to debate the meaning of Jesus's life and death. Some Christian theology considers Jesus's death as redemption because, like freeing a slave by paying ransom, Jesus's death is viewed as a sacrifice or ransom to "buy back" humanity from sin. Other Christians view Jesus's death as further evidence of his opposition to the Romans, and therefore consider Jesus to be the Redeemer because he set people free to gather in his name in opposition to the empire. Rather than placing their trust in the empire, they placed their loyalty to Jesus's teachings and their communities of Jesus followers. Whatever redemptive theology we hold, the enslavement contexts of redemption help us see that referring to one as a servant or slave of God was another way to say they did not belong to an earthly enslaver. Redemption is about being set free.

◇◇◇

Religion

It's always interesting when people deny religion but enthusiastically attend yoga multiple times a week for physical and spiritual satisfaction. To be clear, there are valid reasons to reject expressions of religion for the harm it has done, but the word religion needs reclaiming. Religion and yoga share spiritual and linguistic elements. The word *religion* comes from the Latin root *religare*, which means "to tie or bind together." The word *yoga* comes from an Indo-European root for "to join together." Yoga, like religion, seeks to realign, or bring together—similar to the way ligaments join our bones together for a purpose. Religious spaces, including those used for church and yoga, bring together what would otherwise be separate, contributing to a sense of wholeness. Religion brings people together in structured and ritualistic ways.

Our capitalistic values of efficiency, growth, competition, and self-interest lead us to believe that experience is all external and individual. However, religion at its best seeks to unite our internal and external experiences by incorporating community, mind, body, emotion, and spirit. Religion, at its best, contains gatherings, liturgies, and rituals to bind parts of us together that would otherwise be separate.

Many people prefer yoga to church, and perhaps understandably so given the harm done in the name of Christianity. However, if Christianity, and religion at large, takes accountability for the destruction, it must also be recognized for the acts of compassion, love, and charity done in its name. Education, music, art, social networks, and providing food, shelter, and other assistance have all been connected to religion and provided to those within and outside the church over the centuries. Religion, while undeniably harmful and destructive in some respects, is also the root of much good in the world.

Linguists debate the etymological roots of the word *religion*. For example, Cicero wrote that the Latin *religionem* comes from *relegere*, which means to reread something, pointing to reading religious texts again and again. Cicero's linguistic origin is unlikely, but others suggest that the word *religens* is opposite from *negligens*, which means to neglect; so religion would therefore mean to be purposeful. To live religiously would be to live intentionally. No matter the linguistic origins, for many religion is about wholeness and intentionality.

Repentance

The words *repent* and *redeem* are often discussed in relation to sin. Simply put, when we repent, we are redeemed. In other words, when we take accountability for our wrongs or sins, we are forgiven and set free. Repentance often involves a confession of some sort, but the manner of confession varies widely among Christians.

The etymology of the word *repent* is telling. The Hebrew word that is often translated into English as repent or repentance is *tshuvah*, which means "to turn, to return." This makes sense when we think about a primary portion of the storyline in the Hebrew Bible—Babylonian exile. Ancient Israel returns home where God is. This is what it means to repent—to return to God. For the Israelites, this meant leaving exile and returning to a physical home. This can also be understood metaphorically. "Home" can be anywhere or any state of being where we find peace, comfort, love, and God. When we are separated from this, to repent and be redeemed is to return to it.

Rabbi Danya Ruttenberg says this about repentance: "Judaism doesn't emphasize forgiveness to the same degree that Christianity and secular American society do. Jewish law teaches that the person harmed is certainly not obligated to forgive a perpetrator who has not done the work of repentance."[35] Repentance is work. It is a process entered into both to account for the harm done and to transform the self into one who does not do harm. Repentance requires deep transformation.

In the New Testament, the Greek verb *metanoeite* (Matthew 3:2, Matthew 4:17, and Mark 1:15) means to go beyond the mind we have or to see things with a different perspective and in a more expanded way. St. Jerome translated this word into Latin as *paenitentia*, meaning to "repent" or "do penance." Looking at the original Greek shifts how we may interpret these texts. For example, in Mark 1:15, Jesus says that the kingdom of God is near and we should repent. He is not telling his followers that they must fall to their knees in confession and be in a state of remorse for their sins, although this could be part of the process of repentance. He is also saying they must expand their ways of seeing because the kingdom of God, or a new kind of life beyond Roman occupation, is coming.

Without repentance, we remain stuck in a cycle of causing harm—collectively and individually. Any liberating spiritual path includes practices and rituals pertaining to repentance. Repentance is not about forgiving when we are wronged, but is instead about being held

35. Danya Ruttenberg, *On Repentance and Repair: Making Amends in an Unapologetic World* (Boston, MA: Beacon Press, 2022), 24.

accountable when we do wrong, knowingly or unknowingly. It is about being in right relationship with God and with other humans. Repentance is a process for individuals, communities, organizations, and nations. If this process is not completed, harm will continue to be in circulation, in one way or another, until it is dealt with. This is the nature of reality. It is true in our personal lives, and it is true in the history of a nation. In the Jewish tradition, it is emphasized during Yom Kippur and the High Holy Days; however, it is seen as a lifelong commitment and process.

In many Christian services, especially within liturgical denominations, the community participates in a communal confession of sin, shares the peace of Christ, and then participates in the Eucharist or Holy Communion. This liturgical order reflects the process of repentance: confession, reconciliation or restitution, and communion with God. Theologically, this order of events in worship emphasizes that we cannot commune with God in the form of the Eucharist if we are not first in right relationship with our neighbors.

In repentance, especially in the Jewish tradition that Jesus was a part of, we are not exempt from responsibility for the sins of those who came before us. Increasingly, church liturgies include the acknowledgement of our ancestors' sins in the prayers of confession. This liturgical practice contradicts our modern cultural value of individualism; it may even be difficult to swallow. Yet harm continues to circulate, recycle, and recur across generations until it is repented and reconciliation is sought. Repentance transcends time in this way.

Although repentance is often framed as a form of individual guilt, at its best repentance is about transformation and structural change. Repentance is not a symbolic act of empty words, but a true turning around from wrongdoing and transforming future actions through practical means. Churches today that acknowledge their ancestors' sins—the sin of American slavery, for example, and the sin of colonization—begin to practice their confession by understanding Christianity's role in justifying these sins. Acknowledging this theological heritage, especially for white Christians, continues with the recognition of its ongoing impact through systems that continue to uphold the legacy of racial injustice. Repentance then must take up the work of reconciliation, which may involve paying for material reparations, changing political policy to right wrongs, or joining efforts to stop harmful behavior from continuing.

Systems of chattel slavery in the United States have been abolished, but modern capitalism is still responsible for other forms of enslavement, including exploitative wages and prison labor. Global supply chains rely on unethically low wages and subjugating work conditions. Ultimately, repentance is about transformation. This means true repentance must include the dismantling of oppressive economic systems that continue to exploit people. Harm will continue until we repent together and intentionally transform our social systems. There is no other way.

The nature of continuous harm has surfaced in psychology and therapy discourse recently with the discussion of generational trauma, and how to interrupt its cycle. People are beginning to recognize—or rather remember—that the harm done before our time follows us into our time. The behaviors of our grandparents impacted the childhoods of our parents, which in turn play a central role in our lives today. There is no clear separation between past, present, and future. Accountability must be taken somewhere along the line. Repentance is needed. The trauma remains in circulation until someone takes accountability and refuses to keep it in motion. Repentance is not a temporary, one-and-done, individual process. It is an ongoing process and a way of life.

◇◇◇

Ritual

As part of my doctoral research, I interviewed a woman who had left the evangelical church of her childhood. She was accustomed to praise bands, hundreds of people swaying with arms raised towards the ceiling, and tears falling from many eyes. Her pastor gave forty-minute sermons that left the congregation in an emotional state, usually angry, guilty, or self-righteous. She told me the first time she worshipped at a mainline Protestant church, she was bored. Nobody cried. The music was less performative and more organic, with out-of-tune singing. The pastor's sermon was short and did not stir up intense emotions among the parishioners. After a few months of attending this new church, she realized what she'd perceived as boredom was actually safety.

The truth is most people's lives are not a series of dramatic events, one after the other. We all have more intense stages of life where everything changes suddenly: graduations, marriages, having children, loss of a loved one, divorces, addictions, illness, etc. However, most of our lives consist of the mundane, repetitive moments of making our beds, doing the dishes, choosing produce at the store, doing yard work, commuting to and from work, meetings, etc. These small rituals, strung together over time, make up our lives.

The earliest Jesus followers debated more about having the right rituals than the right beliefs. In fact, in the first and second centuries, Jesus communities found orthopraxy, correct conduct and liturgy, more important than orthodoxy, the correct belief and doctrine. Rituals at their core are deeply human. Rituals make up a liturgical life. Liturgy teaches us that this repetition is holy, if we give it intention and attention. A pattern of behavior or activity is not in itself sacred, but is made that way by associating it with the divine. Doing the dishes, mowing the lawn, or taking the bus can be set aside and made holy, if we are intentional about it. And when these rituals are made sacred, they become the liturgies of our lives.

◇◇◇

Sabbath

For the Israelites wandering in the desert, time was measured by sunrises, sunsets, phases of the moon, and seasons. In fact, these methods of measuring time shaped the Hebrew language. The Hebrew word for *month* is *yerach*, which comes from the Hebrew word for moon. *Rosh Chodesh* means "head of the month," a holiday observed at the beginning of each month or, in ancient times, to celebrate a new moon and make offerings. Because the Jewish calendar marks the beginning of a new day at sunset, Shabbat—or Sabbath—begins Friday evening after the sun sets and ends on Saturday at sunset.

Sabbath observation is one of the Ten Commandments: remember the Sabbath day, and keep it holy. Moses liberated the Israelites from their enslaved labor in Egypt, and they became a nation of nomads. What good is liberation if you don't remind yourself to enjoy it? The Sabbath is a weekly reminder to enjoy liberation. We can imagine the gift of a regular practice of Sabbath for a group of people who had recently been slave laborers in Egypt for multiple generations.

Sabbath is a sanctuary in time rather than space[36]—understandable for a community who spent so many years in the wilderness. They did not have physical places of worship, so Sabbath became a space of worship implanted in time. Sabbath could not be taken, destroyed, or con-

36. Abraham Joshua Herschel, *The Sabbath: Its Meaning for Modern Man* (New York: Farrah, Straus and Giroux, 1951), 8.

quered. In fact, Hebrew consciousness understood time to be just as much a space in reality as physical space, and we can see this in the Hebrew language. In biblical Hebrew, there is no word that translated directly as "thing." The word *davar* came to be used for "thing" later on, but the meaning of *davar* ranged from something like a message, report, promise, advice, or decision. Ancient Hebrew's lack of a direct word for "thing" demonstrates the Hebrew ability to view reality as not only materialistic, so Sabbath was easily seen as a space existing outside of material reality.

Shavat means "to stop." The Greek word *sabbaton* can be traced to the Hebrew word *shabbat*, which is where we get *Sabbath* and *sabbatical.* All of this is to say that Shabbat, or the Sabbath, has everything to do with stopping—more specifically, stopping our labors for a given amount of time. Jewish theologians often make the point that Sabbath is not about resting because of exhaustion but about stopping our labor to enjoy God's creation.[37] For many, we have become so occupied by our work in the world that we forget we are liberated, even if our work is enjoyable. The Sabbath was important to the liberation of ancient Israelites, and it continues to be about liberation for us today.

Rest is likewise essential to liberation, as demonstrated by theologian Tricia Hersey, the founder of The Nap Ministry, an organization encouraging rest as a form of resistance. Resisting the impulse labor around the clock—and resisting the definition of our existence through our labor—is resisting the capitalist machine. Oppression and labor always hold hands. As an anti-power practice, Hersey encourages, slow down. Stop responding to emails immediately, take breaks from social media, avoid the hamster wheel of production, reject grind culture, listen and connect. If we are liberated, we must have rituals in place to consistently remind us that freedom is to exist outside of toxic systems.

37. Faydra L. Shapiro and Len Woods, *Romance Behind Judaica: Celebrating the Richness of the Jewish Calendar* (Brentwood, TN: Worthy Books, 2019), 16.

Liberation and oppression are felt in our bones. They are embodied experiences. Oppressive beliefs like theologies justifying the need for women to avoid leadership roles feel like control, and control is always a mask for fear. On the other hand, liberation feels like nothing to prove and no ladder to climb. Oppression is labored breathing, while liberation is a slow, deep, calming breath. Oppression is rushed and urgent, while liberation compels us to take our time or forget time altogether. Oppression is forced production, while liberation is choosing connection. Liberation is rest. Liberation is Sabbath. We know it when we feel it.

Liberation is here and now, not an exodus from the here and now. Sabbath teaches us how to experience this spiritual liberation. Sabbath is practice for the world to come. For Christians, Communion or Eucharist is also a foretaste of what is to come. Sabbath is practicing this recognition of peace on earth, and it is a practice of being present in time.

Sabbath is an intentional rejection of the systems that dominate and our roles within these systems. The Sabbath is about avoiding distractions and the desire to dominate in order to sink into the awareness of eternity. In Genesis 2:1–3, God rested on the seventh day. While Sabbath is often about resting, resting is a secondary aspect to the cessation of labor. The more important part of Sabbath is the ceasing of labor. Rest can occur when labor stops.

◇◇◇

Sacred

The word *sacred* comes from the Latin *sacer* or *sacrare*, meaning "consecrated" or "set apart for the gods." This is also connected to the root word for sacrifice. *Sacer*, referring to something set apart from the mundane and therefore revered or feared, can imply danger or curse;

this dual meaning has been largely lost in English connotations of the word *sacred*.

To set something apart as sacred requires an intentional act of meaning making. For example, I have recently been doing dishes by hand rather than using the dish washer to have a few minutes each day of quiet embodiment. I am making these moments sacred by giving them deeper meaning compared to other moments in my day.

In Jewish and Christian contexts, the sacred is associated with God's presence. In Judaism, this meant in the Temple. In today's Christianity, it often means through the Eucharist. Similarly, spaces, texts, rites, and objects are considered sacred because they are intentionally set apart from the profane, meaning common.

Of course, those with political power have historically been able to decide what was considered sacred. The priesthood and clergy have long been considered sacred positions of authority. Reformers like Martin Luther questioned this by emphasizing the "priesthood of all believers," meaning he argued that clergy were not the only sacred people within the Church. As a result, the Bible was translated into vernacular languages. This could be viewed as blurring the line between the sacred and profane, or as reclaiming what is sacred as also accessible to common people.

A hard line between what is sacred and what is not has often reinforced power structures. Jesus himself challenged traditional notions of sacredness by healing on the Sabbath and touching what was considered to be unclean. Jesus challenged rigid sacred boundaries, and the Church has a history of sometimes enforcing these hard lines. What is considered sacred is always in negotiation. Meaning always lies where humans put it, so we should be intentional about what we deem as sacred.

Salvation

Linguistically, salvation relates to the Latin *salvare* meaning "to save," and *salvere* meaning "to heal." This is also where we get the word *salve*. Interestingly, the words for heal and whole come from the same root as holy, suggesting that these are all related to living a whole life.

The Hebrew verb "to judge" also means "to save." We see this in Psalm 43:1 when David cries out, asking God to judge him. He is asking to be saved. We see the connection between judgment, justice, and salvation in the Hebrew Bible when God is referred to as Judge (Genesis 18:25, Judges 11:27, Isaiah 33:22, and Psalm 94:2) and when God is discussed in relationship to judgment (Psalm 89:14). Additionally, Isaiah uses the word *judgment* to discuss salvation.

There is a long history of those in power parading as both judges and saviors. As we have seen, savior was a common title given to Roman emperors because it was their responsibility to save people from the dangers of life. While the empire did save people from pirates, it caused more danger for those they conquered than protection. Despite the propaganda that the emperor provided salvation, people realized that the emperor did not provide the salvation they needed to survive and thrive. They needed another source of salvation.

Salvation in the Bible and for the early Jesus communities had little to do with the afterlife. In fact, the ancient Israelites did not believe in an afterlife. For Israelites, salvation was rarely about being saved from your sins. Instead, it was about liberation from Egyptian bondage and returning home from Babylonian exile. God saved God's people from Egyptian and Babylonian oppression, and this salvation continued in ancient Israel's radical socioeconomic structure with no interest charged on loans, debts forgiven every seven years, a jubilee year every half century when agriculture land was returned to its original owners or their family. These laws were to ensure that the system did not favor the wealthy while oppressing those in poverty. For early communities of Jesus followers, they turned towards these small communities for the support and salvation the Roman Empire failed to provide; in this way, church communities can be seen as a source of salvation.

Christians have many ways of understanding and experiencing salvation. Marcus J. Borg summarizes the multitude of understandings of salvation as being about: liberation from bondage, including economic and political bondage; as a return from exile, or a coming home; as moving from death to life, like a "born again" experience; as infirmity to well-being, meaning being healed from something; or as moving from fear to trust, meaning being rid of anxiety and worry.

I heard a Buddhist once say that when he meditates, he reaches the edge of enlightenment. He can only approach the edge because there is no full enlightenment at an individual level. He would have to turn around and bring all of creation with him. Enlightenment, akin to what many Christians mean when they say "salvation," is communal, which is to say that it extends beyond personal salvation and into the realm of politics, justice, and peace.

The title of savior was later transferred to Jesus by his early followers. In fact, *Yeshua* in Hebrew means "to rescue" or "salvation." The idea that salvation came from Jesus was deeply countercultural. To believe that salvation came through Jesus, the tortured and crucified, rather than through the emperor was a bold statement against the Roman Empire. Viewing salvation in this cultural context provides a framework that allows us to see salvation as both a personal and communal liberation. Salvation, at its core, is about safety from what oppresses us, individually and collectively.

◇◇◇

Sign of the Cross

Literacy is not simply about reading words on a page. Literacy is anything that conveys meaning, like the sign of the cross. In this way, there is more to Christian literacy than the words in the Bible.

Early Christians traced a small cross on their foreheads, a reference to Ezekiel 9:7.[38] That mark was both a cross and the Greek letter *tau*, written as *T* and standing for the name of God. Early Christians quickly adopted these cross symbols, as evident from the teachings of Tertullian, Justin Martyr, Origen, and Jerome. By the third century, Jesus followers were also tracing the small sign on their lips, on their breasts, and in the air as a blessing over people and things, as many Christians still do today. Over time, the pattern of the cross shifted. In the Western Church, the sign of the cross went from the forehead to breast, left shoulder to right shoulder, and then center of the breast. In the Eastern Church, however, instead of moving from left to right shoulder, they go from the right to the left.

The development of the larger sign of the cross extending from our foreheads to our chest and shoulders may have had to do with the Monophysite heresy in the seventh and eighth centuries. Monophysites were members of a fifth-century Christian theological movement; they believed that Christ was only divine in nature. Their belief was in direct contrast to a Christian doctrine formulated by the Council of Chalcedon in 451 CE, which states that Jesus the Christ had two natures—divine and human. This debate impacted the way Christians made the sign of the cross. Those who believed in the single nature of Christ—divine only—would make a large sign of the cross with only their index finger,

38. Billy Kangas, "Where Did the Sign of the Cross Come From?" *Patheos*, February 13, 2021, https://www.patheos.com/blogs/billykangas/2012/02/where-did-the-sign-of-the-cross-come-from.html.

so it was visible to others that they believed in the single nature of Christ. Those who believed in the dual nature of Christ—divine and human—would make a large sign of the cross with two fingers, symbolizing Christ's two natures. These two ways of making the cross sign was a silent representation over a theological dispute. The Monophysites were deemed heretics, and the mainstream Church adopted the dual nature of Christ.

Differing opinions about the sign of the cross continue to be discussed today. Some Protestant Christians refuse to make the sign of the cross because they think this symbol belongs only to the Catholic Church. However, the sign of the cross is practiced by many Lutherans, Episcopalians, and other mainline Protestants. Like our spoken vocabulary, the silent gesture of making a sign of the cross has a different meaning to different Christians who use it (and who don't).

Sin

THE WORD FOR SIN can mean "to miss the mark." For example, Judges 20:16 discusses slinging a stone in the air and not missing. The Hebrew word for "miss" in this context is *khata*, which is the same word meaning to sin. However, the word *sin* is not always used in an abstract context in the Hebrew Bible. Sin is often discussed using the Hebrew word *nasa*, which means to lift or carry (see Genesis 4:13, Exodus 19:4, and Ezekiel 23:49).

Dominant forms of Christianity in the West have a problematic conception of sin. They overemphasize individual guilt and have often weaponized the notion of sin as a tool of social control. In many dominant Christian frameworks, sin is connected to bodily desires related to sexuality, often causing repression and harm. Sin is sometimes viewed through a dualistic lens, creating false binaries like right and wrong, or good and evil. Sin is an important word that needs reclaiming, while including the ethical and moral complexities of the human condition.

The concept of original sin is not biblical either, but was introduced by Augustine in the fifth century. The notion that original sin is the cause of human suffering can lead to harmful results, but Augustine's doctrine of original sin is not without criticism.[39]

Despite mainstream Christianity's understanding of sin, Jews and early Jesus followers, many of whom were Jews, had a different understanding. There are, of course, individual sins that we need to recognize, confess, and seek forgiveness for. However, our individualistic society tends to focus on only individual sins. Enslaved in Egypt, in Babylonian exile, and then living under the oppression of the Roman Empire, the Jewish people understood the evils of collective corporate sin. The Bible speaks about this collective sin as it is present in institutions, nations, and systems. Micah 1:5 discusses the sins as they relate to Samaria and Jerusalem, capitals of kingdoms that ruled and dominated.

With the cultural and linguistic context in mind, we can see how religion, bringing holy living and salvation into community, can be the antidote to the sin that brings fragmentation to our lives. While Christianity may include a focus on a life beyond this one, this has not been the understanding for a majority of history. Christianity offers transformation here and now, for individuals and the collective whole. We all desire liberation from something, and that is what the Christian story offers.

39. Matthew Fox, *Original Blessing* (New York: Jeremy P. Tarcher/Putnam, 2000).

Tithing

THE WORD *TITHING* COMES from the Old English term *teogotha*, which means "a tenth." This word derives from the Proto-Germanic root *tehun*, which simply means ten. There is biblical precedence for the practice of tithing. In the context of the Hebrew Bible, Genesis 14:20 discusses Melchizedek blessing Abram and then says, "Abram gave him one-tenth of everything." The Hebrew word for tithes is *ma'aser*, which literally means one-tenth. Additionally, Genesis 28:22 states Jacob tells God he will give one-tenth to God. These verses have been used to support the practice of tithing.

Tithing is the mandate or expectation that ten percent of one's income is to be given to the church or synagogue. Tithing has a complicated history. During Jesus's lifetime, peasants who were struggling to make ends meet under Roman occupation were required to pay what is referred to as triple taxation—their taxes, tribute to the Romans, and a tithe to the Temple.

Tithing was an institutionalized practice in Second Temple Judaism, and in early medieval England, tithing was a legal requirement. In our individualized and profit-driven economy, this expectation outrages many people. However, tithing is a way for the church, or Temple, to pay those who keep the organization running and to help the poor. Of course, tithing becomes problematic when the practice is abused to create wealthy religious leaders, as is the case today in many churches and was the case in the Temple during Jesus's time.

Acknowledging the harm of enforced tithing is important, but tithing carries spiritual and communal benefits, too. Monetary tithing is not the only way to give to a church community. Giving, monetarily or otherwise, is what it means to be part of a community.

Churches following in the teachings of Jesus are tasked with feeding the hungry and helping the poor. This requires resources. Jesus taught against the attachment to wealth, and tithing is a practice that helps to avoid being attached to our personal wealth. Tithing, at its core, is about knowing that what we have is not ours to hoard or protect, but instead is to give freely and share. Tithing is an ethic of communal reciprocity, which is countercultural in a society attached to the accumulation of wealth.

TRINITY

A STRONG EXAMPLE of the fact that the Bible does not contain the entirety of the developed and developing Christian faith is the word *Trinity*. This word cannot be found in the Bible.

Paul helped set some groundwork for the idea of the Trinity. Paul elevated Jesus to the status of God often, and traces of Trinitarian theology can be found in 2 Corinthians 13:13 when he writes: "The grace of the Lord Jesus Christ, the love of God, and the communion of the Holy Spirit be with all of you."

However, during the first century, there was no formal understanding of the Trinity, a church teaching defining God as three entities in one essence, Father, Son, Holy Spirit. Matthew 28:19 does mention baptizing in the name of Father, Son, and Holy Spirit, but the fully realized doctrine of the Trinity does not begin to be articulated until Emperor Constantine supports Christianity in the early fourth century. In 325 CE, Constantine convened the Council of Nicaea to resolve theological disputes, including the argument around Jesus's divine identity. The Council of Nicaea created the Nicene Creed to unify Christianity, a step toward an official Trinitarian doctrine.

In 381 CE, the Council of Constantinople expanded the Nicene Creed and affirmed the divinity of the Holy Spirit. Multiple theologians over a few centuries, like Augustine of Hippo, helped form and refine the doctrine of the Trinity. The Councils of Nicaea and Constantinople were brought about through the Emperor Constantine. Constantine wanted a unified Christianity, and this began with understanding, and in some ways deciding, Jesus's identity. This is not to deny the truth found in the Trinity, but power has influenced the precise ways we discuss, think, and visualize the Trinity.

Truth

We often equate truth with fact, but linguistically these two words have had separate histories. What is true is not always factual. We can see this difference in the fable of the tortoise and the hare. The slow tortoise races the quick hare and wins the race. This story is not factual, meaning the story is not based on an actual tortoise racing an actual hare at some point in history. Instead, this story reveals a truth—slow and steady wins the race. This story is true without being factual.

The word *fact* comes from the Latin word *facere*, which means "to make," implying that what is deemed factual is made into reality rather than inherent; human beings decide what is factually true through our own processes of knowledge-creation and consensus. For example, the scientific method is a process that helps us decide what is factual, and the scientific method must be applied to the same concept repeatedly until the scientific community will determine a theory or hypothesis to be a fact.

Truth, however, is different. Truth has not always been about believing the correct thing, and instead has had more of a focus on the believer. The word connected to truth in Old English is *triewth* or *treowth*, which means faithfulness and constancy. It is not about what is being believed but rather the process of believing itself. Truth is related to the word *troth*, which refers to loyalty and is often used in the context of marriage and engagement, as in to be betrothed to someone. Additionally, a knight might be described as true or having truth. To be true or have truth meant to be loyal and pledge a certain allegiance to a spouse, God, or nation. The Hebrew word that often gets translated as truth in the Old Testament is *emeth*, which relates to trustworthiness.

For most of Christian history, truth meant to be committed to someone or something, not to possess correct knowledge. Truth could not be proven or argued, but was instead embodied in your character and loyalties. You could be true to God, but not true about God. You were true to someone or something, not about something. The definition of truth began to shift with the invention of the printing press, the Protestant Reformation, Modernism, and the Age of Enlightenment.

Word of God

Many Christians refer to the Bible as the Word of God, and this can be problematic if taken at face value. There are some faithful from across religious traditions who believe their sacred text was whispered directly from God. My branch of Christianity teaches that the Bible is a collection of texts from believers, not a text given to us directly by God. There is humanity in the Bible, and like humanity, it is complicated.

An Alexandrian Jewish philosopher named Philo (25 BCE–50 CE) contributed to the notion that early Christian writers could think philosophically about biblical doctrines. One of these ideas was the *logos*, which is often translated as "Word" and refers to the divine reason present in the world. Readings of the discussion of this Word of God, or *Logos* in John 1:1–18 have argued that Jesus is the divine reason present in the world. Therefore, Christian belief places Jesus as the Word of God, existing at the beginning and dwelling in the man of Jesus of Nazareth.

CONCLUSION

When I first began attending church as an adult, I remember feeling like I was entering one giant book club that was taking place all around the world. People were connecting over and debating about this ancient story, and I was excited to join the conversation.

A few years ago, I met a young woman who was a lifelong Christian. We talked about the Bible, and when I enthusiastically told her about the books I was reading and what I had been learning about Christianity, she told me that people who need to go beyond the Bible to understand the Bible had a "low view of scripture." She went on to say that she and her church have a "high view of scripture," and therefore need nothing but the Bible to know Jesus.

I entertained her belief that the Bible alone could transform. With high hopes, I read the entire Bible from Genesis to Revelation. I didn't get it. More than that, I was left profoundly confused.

It wasn't until I began to learn about the social and political contexts of various biblical writings and communities that I found myself able to read the Bible and become immersed in the story. I began to understand that the Bible is not an isolated collection of moral teachings or spiritual truths, but instead a collection of texts responding to experienced systems of oppression—empires, enslavement, economic injustices. I came to realize that Christianity is not a passive belief system but an active engagement with this world. Christianity positions God not as a distant ruler but as a force aligned with the marginalized and oppressed among us. A little bit at a time, I was transformed.

I do not have a "low view of scripture." I have a serious view of scripture that incorporates the paradox, nuance, and complexity of this ancient collection of sacred texts. I love language, and I love the story of Jesus. To write a book about the language we use to tell the story of Jesus, both in the Bible and in church, is my way of fully entering the ongoing Christian conversation. It's my hope to support your serious and ever-deepening understanding of the Bible, too, as part of your faith.

Christianity is a work in progress. It always has been. We gather around this story using both the text and church rituals, and we wrestle with what it all means. Together, we construct meaning, just like they did in the various councils of the early church, just as biblical scholars and translators have done for centuries. In academia, the belief that knowledge is co-constructed through our communities and cultures is called social constructivism. I am a social constructivist. The way we infuse meaning into Christian words and phrases is socially constructed, as evident by the ways various Christians use the same words to mean different things. When I say I have experienced salvation, that means something very different to different Christians. The language we use to tell the story continues to be negotiated and constructed.

This is where the church comes in. The Bible needs the Church, and the Church needs the Bible. We gather regularly. We connect. We disagree. We change. We debate. This is what it has always meant to be Christian: entering into the conversation. I want to be a part of this conversation.

SOURCES

Ajoy, April. *Star-Spangled Jesus: Leaving Christian Nationalism and Finding a True Faith*. Worthy Publishing, 2024.

Aslan, Reza. *Zealot: The Life and Times of Jesus of Nazareth*. Random House, 2013.

Balentine, Samuel E. *Leviticus: Interpretation: A Bible Commentary for Teaching and Preaching*. Westminster John Knox Press, 2011.

Barton, John. *A History of the Bible: The Book & Its Faiths*. Penguin Books, 2020.

Barton, John. *The Word: How We Translate the Bible—And Why it Matters*. Basic Books, 2023.

Bass, Diana Butler. "Sending the Goose." Wild Goose Festival. 2022 July 17. https://youtu.be/sSH-nfdh_S0?si=2n-fBcPbjZsNwJsd

Bell, Rob. "Blood, Guts & Fire: The Gospel According to Leviticus." https://robbell.com/audio/blood-guts-and-fire-leviticus/

Bell, Rob. "Jesus, Domitian and The Book of Revelation." YouTube video, posted by John JP Patterson, May 16, 2018.

Bell, Rob, *Love Wins: A Book About Heaven, Hell, and the Fate of Every Person Who Ever Lived*. HarperOne, 2012.

Bell, Rob. *What Is the Bible?: How an Ancient Library of Poems, Letters, and Stories Can Transform the Way You Think and Feel About Everything*. HarperOne, 2017.

Benckhuysen, Amanda W. *The Gospel According to Eve: A History of Women's Interpretation*. InterVarsity Press, 2019.

Bergsma, John. *Jesus and the Jubilee: The Biblical Roots of the Year of God's Favor*. Emmaus Road Publishing, 2025.

Bivin, David, and Roy Blizzard Jr. *Understanding the Difficult Words of Jesus: New Insights from a Hebrew Perspective*. Destiny Image Publishers, 1994.

Borg, Marcus J. *Speaking Christian: Why Christian Words Have Lost Their Power and How They Can Be Restored*. HarperCollins Publishers, 2011.

Borg, Marcus J., and John Dominic Crossan. *The Last Week: What the Gospels Really Teach About Jesus's Final Days in Jerusalem*. HarperOne, 2007.

Borowski, Oded. *Every Living Thing: Daily Use of Animals in Ancient Israel*. AltaMira Press, 1998.

Brueggemann, Walter. *The Prophetic Imagination: 40th Anniversary Edition*. Fortress Press, 2018.

Burrus, Virginia. "The Gender of Martyrdom," paper presented at the Westar Institute Annual Meeting, Christian Seminary (Denver, CO). November 2018.

Cahill, Thomas. *Desire of the Everlasting Hills: The World Before and After Jesus*. Nan A. Talese/Anchor Books, 1999.

Cahill, Thomas. *The Gifts of the Jews: How a Tribe of Desert Nomads Changed the Way Everyone Thinks and Feels*. Nan A. Talese/Anchor Books, 1998.

Clifton, Chas S. *Encyclopedia of Heresies and Heretics*. ABC-CLIO, 1992.

Coates, Jennifer. *Women, Men and Language: A Sociolinguistic Account of Gender Differences in Language*. Longman, 2004.

Danker, Frederick W. *Benefactor: Epigraphic Study of a Graeco-Roman and New Testament Semantic Field*. Clayton Publishing House, 1982.

Eberle, Gary. *Dangerous Words: Talking about God in an Age of Fundamentalism*. Trumpeter, 2007.

Eusebius. "The Letter of the Churches of Vienne and Lyon." *Eusebius' Ecclesiastical History*, Volume 1. Hendrickson Publishers, 1998.

Garnsey, Peter. *Food and Society in Classical Antiquity*. Cambridge University Press, 1999.

Gleason, Maud W. *Making Men: Sophists and Self-Presentation in Ancient Rome*. Princeton University Press, 1995.

Herman, Bart D. *Armageddon: What the Bible Really Says About the End*. Simon & Schuster, 2023.

Herschel, Abraham Joshua. *The Sabbath: It's Meaning for Modern Man*. Farrah, Straus and Giroux, 1951.

Hersey, Tricia. *Rest is Resistance: A Manifesto*. Hachette Book Group, 2022.

Janz, Denis R., editor. *A People's History of Christianity Student Edition: From the Early Church to the Reformation, Volume 1*. Fortress Press, 2014.

Kelly, Henry Ansgar. "Adam Citings before the Intrusion of Satan: Recontextualizing Paul's Theology of Sin and Death." *Biblical Theology Bulletin*, Volume 44: Number 1, 2014.

Klein, Patricia S. *Worship Without Words: The Signs and Symbols of Our Faith*. Paraclete Press, 2000.

Levine, Amy-Jill. *Sermon on the Mount: A Beginner's Guide to the Kingdom of Heaven*. Abingdon Press, 2020.

Levine, Amy-Jill and Marc Zvi Brettler. *The Bible With and Without Jesus: How Jews and Christians Read the Same Stories Differently*. HarperOne, 2023.

McClellan, Dan. *The Bible Says So: What We Get Right (and Wrong) About Scripture's Most Controversial Issues*. St. Martin's Essentials, 2025.

McClellan, Dan, and Dan Beecher. "The Blessing of the Magdalene with Elizabeth Schrader Polczer." *Data Over Dogma*. Podcast. June 26, 2023.

McClellan, Dan, and Dan Beecher. "The Case of the Missing Verses." *Data Over Dogma*. Podcast. July 31, 2023.

McWhorter, John. *Nine Nasty Words: English in the Gutter: Then, Now, and Forever*. Avery, 2021.

Melnikov, F.E. "The Sign of the Cross," *The Old Believers*. Substack, https://oldbeliever.substack.com/p/the-sign-of-the-cross. November *9, 2023*

Merritt, Jonathan. *Learning to Speak God from Scratch*. New York: Convergent, 2018.

Meshorer, Ya'akov. *Treasury of Jewish Coins from the Persian Period to Bar Kokhba*. Amphora Books, 2001.

Montell, Amanda. Cultish: *The Language of Fanaticism*. Harper Wave, 2021.

Montell, Amanda. *Wordslut: A Feminist Guide to Taking Back the English Language*. Harper Wave, 2019.

Moss, Candida. *God's Ghostwriters: Enslaved Christians and the Making of the Bible*. Little, Brown and Company, 2024.

Musurillo, H. R., translator. *The Passion of Ss. Perpetua and Felicitas*. Colorado College. Accessed on https://cdn.inst-fs-iad-prod.inscloudgate.net/

Nuttall, Jenni. *Mother Tongue: The Surprising History of Women's Words*. Penguin Random House, 2023.

Plank, Liz. *For the Love of Men: From Toxic to a More Mindful Masculinity*. Griffin, 2021.

Parrott, D. M., translator. *The Sophia of Jesus Christ*. The Nag Hammadi Library. Accessed on http://www.gnosis.org/naghamm/sjc.html

Richards, E. Randolph, and Brandon J. O'Brien. *Misreading Scripture with Western Eyes: Removing Cultural Blinders to Better Understand the Bible*. IVP Books, 2012.

Robert, Dana L. *Christian Mission: How Christianity Became a World Religion*. Wiley-Blackwell, 2009.

Rohr, Richard. *The Tears of Things: Prophetic Wisdom for an Age of Outrage*. Convergent Books, 2025.

Rohr, Richard. *The Universal Christ: How a Forgotten Reality Can Change Everything We See, Hope For, and Believe*. Convergent, 2021.

Ruttenberg, Danya. *On Repentance and Repair: Making Amends in an Unapologetic World*. Beacon Press, 2022.

Schlimm, Matthew Richard. *70 Hebrew Words Every Christian Should Know*. Abingdon Press, 2018.

Schrader Polczer, Elizabeth. "'Those Who Love Me Will Keep My Word': Narrative Variants in New Testament Gospel Stories." PhD dissertation. Duke University, 2023.

Shapiro, Faydra L., and Len Woods. *Romance Behind Judaica: Celebrating the Richness of the Jewish Calendar*. Worthy Books, 2019.

Stauffer, Ethelbert. *Christ and the Caesars: Historical Sketches*. Wipf & Stock, 1952.

Tabick, Jacqueline. "The Snake in the Grass: The Problems of Interpreting Symbols in the Hebrew Bible and Rabbinic Writings," *Religion* 16 (2), 1986.

Tertullian of Carthage, *Martyrdom of St. Perpetua and Felicity*, translated by R E Wallis. Dalcassian Publishing Company, 2023.

Torjesen, Karen Jo. *When Women Were Priests: Women's Leadership in the Early Church & the Scandal of their Subordination in the Rise of Christianity*. HarperCollins, 1993.

Totelin, Laurence. "Old Recipes, New Practice? The Latin Adaptations of the Hippocratic Gynaecological Treatises," *Social History of Medicine*. Volume 24, No. 1, 2011.

Vearncombe, Erin K., Bernard Brandon Scott, and Hal Taussig. *After Jesus Before Christianity: A Historical Exploration of the First Two Centuries of Jesus Movements*. HarperOne, 2021.

Whitaker, Robyn J. *Revelation for Normal People: A Guide to the Strangest and Most Dangerous Book in the Bible*. The Bible for Normal People, 2023.

ACKNOWLEDGMENTS

LIKE FAITH, writing a book is not a solitary act, but instead requires community and support.

Thank you to the entire team at The Pilgrim Press, including Katie Martin, Adam Bresnahan, and Rev. Rachel Hackenberg. Thank you to Nancy Bryan for the vision, expertise, and countless hours of labor you put into this book.

Thank you to the church communities who let me wrestle shamelessly with the Jesus story out loud over all these years. The adult group at Zion Lutheran Church in Tamaqua, Pennsylvania, who met weekly in 2018 and 2019 to learn about how the Bible came to be, lit a spark in me that led me to writing this book. St. Paul's Lutheran Church in Enola, Pennsylvania is a special place full of special people; thank you for all of the conversations and letting me ask all of my questions. Thank you to St. John's Lutheran Church in Tamaqua, Pennsylvania for being my home from the time my first-born was three weeks old.

Thank you Kristy, Ike, Charyl, and Joe for being wonderful grandparents to my children and the countless hours you all spent with them while I worked on this book. Thank you to my very best friend, Erin, for our friendship, the headshot, and the fact that you will definitely purchase this book even though the topic is of little interest to you.

A very big shout out to Tabitha and Sophia. Tabitha spent many hours coloring next to me at my desk while I wrote this book. Sophia spent many hours climbing all over me while I wrote this book. May you both grow up knowing words are powerful and questions are holy.

Thank you the most to Dillon, who listened to me read every chapter of every draft out loud multiple times, and who helped me protect my morning writing hours for years. Are you free Friday night?

ABOUT THE AUTHOR

Dr. Samantha Bise is a writer who studies Christian language and culture, especially as it relates to themes of power and liberation. She teaches English and social science courses at Penn State Lehigh Valley, Penn State Hazleton, and Lehigh Carbon Community College, and holds a doctorate from Indiana University in literacy, culture, and language education. She takes and audits courses at United Lutheran Seminary because that's her idea of a good time. Samantha lives in Pennsylvania and is the co-creator of a marriage, two tiny humans, and the Church Chatter Podcast.